A

GRAMMAR

OF THE

GUJARATI LANGUAGE

A

GRAMMAR

OF THE

GUJARATI LANGUAGE;

BY

WILLIAM CLARKSON

GYAN

Published by

GYAN

Gyan Publishing House
5, Ansari Road
Daryaganj, New Delhi-110002
Phone: 011-47034999, 9811692060
E-mail: books@gyanbooks.com

Distribution Network
gyanbooks.com
India, USA, Canada, UK, Australia

ISBN: 978-81-212-7077-9 (PB)
First Published, 1847

2nd Impression 2024

Printed at: Gyan Press, Delhi.

A GRAMMAR OF THE GUJARATI LANGUAGE
Author: WILLIAM CLARKSON

A GRAMMAR OF THE GUJARÁTI LANGUAGE;

BY

WILLIAM CLARKSON,

PROTESTANT MISSIONARY TO GUJARA'T

FROM THE LONDON MISSIONARY SOCIETY.

BOMBAY:

AMERICAN MISSION PRESS.

T. GRAHAM, PRINTER.

1847.

TO

THE REVEREND THE MISSIONARIES

OF WESTERN INDIA,

HONOURED FOR THEIR SUBLIME OFFICE,—ESTEEMED VERY HIGHLY FOR THEIR WORKS' SAKE,—BELOVED IN THE LORD,

This Grammar of the Gujarati Language,

IS DEDICATED BY THEIR FELLOW LABOURER IN THE MINISTRATION OF THE GOSPEL OF OUR LORD JESUS CHRIST,

WM. CLARKSON.

Mission Bungalow,
Baroda Camp, 1817.

PREFACE.

The Author presents this Grammar to the Public, not as a critical or minute digest of the Gujarátì Language but as a practical work, expounding its great principles and copiously illustrating them. The Author, although ignorant of Sanscrit, and only partially acquainted with Mahratta and Hindùstanì, and at the same time suffering from the absence of all effective Native aid, was constrained in the midst of other duties to write this work, by the fact of there being no Grammar extant, sufficiently clear or correct, or illustrative to satisfy the student who might be desirous to become a thorough proficient. It was moreover with the especial desire of assisting the Missionary in his arduous work, that this Grammar was composed. The Author does not challenge criticism in every minute particular, nor does he claim for the work an authoritative character. The press of other more important work prevented his paying minute attention to several subjects, which may be elucidated in a future Edition. He takes this opportunity of expressing his thanks to the American Mission Press for the handsome mode in which the work has been executed, and especially for their diligence in cutting out the types of new letters, single and double—expressly for this work.

Much hitherto remains undone in the department of Orthography. The improvements in this work are to be considered only as specimen of what *may* be done, and not as a determinate fixing of the principles of Gujaráti Orthography.

This can only be a work of time and talent, expended by the Gujaráti Scholar on the operations of the Press itself. He must be present to have the types cut out under his own inspection, before he can present a fixed Orthography.

N. B. The Profits of this work are to be devoted unreservedly to the furtherance of Missionary operations in Gujarát, in connection with the "Baroda Mission." Subscribers therefore, by promoting the sale of this work, will not only encourage Literature, but will be positively promoting the cause of Evangelization of the Heathen. An enlarged sale is on these grounds especially desirable.

A

GRAMMAR

OF THE

GUJARÁTI LANGUAGE.

I. ORTHOGRAPHY.

1. The Gujaráti language is written in two characters. The one is called Bálbodh or Shastrí, the other is called Gujaráti. The latter is but a modified and defective form of the former.

2. The Gujaráti character is used for purposes of correspondence and all mercantile transactions. It is therefore the character with which the people generally are conversant.

Several metrical compositions exist in it and some translations from the Sanscrit.

The Christian Scriptures are also published in it.

3. The Bálbodh character is cultivated by the Brámaṇs. Several literary works have been published in it by the Native Education Society. It is commonly taught in the Government Schools. It promises therefore to become the universal character for the purpose of education in the high branches of literature and science.

4. The Bálbodh alphabet is alone a competent representative of the sounds of the oral language. Its orthography is also uniform.

5. The Gujaráti character is exceedingly defective for the above object, having no appropriate symbols of several sounds which are of common recurrence in the language. Its orthography likewise varies almost in every composition.

6. Hence, it is easy to read in the Bálbodh character, after its alphabet has been once mastered, while it is impossible to read correctly in the Gujaráti without a teacher or a previous knowledge of the oral sounds.

7. The letters of the Bálbodh alphabets are fifty-two. Of these, sixteen are reputed vowels, and thirty-six are consonants, of which ten are aspirates. This reputed number is capable of reduction.

It may be doubted whether ऋ ॠ ऌ ॡ are vowels at all. The anusvara is not strictly a vowel, but the symbol of a nasal sound, which may be attached to any vowel.

The visarg, representing a mere aspirate, is also questionable as a vowel, being the representative of a final ह *ha*. The consonants क्ष ज्ञ are compound, and have no right to insertion in the alphabet.

8. The letters of the Gujaráti as here given are thirty-nine. Of these, nine are vowels inclusive of the point. No fixed number of letters can be assigned, inasmuch as Bálbodh letters are now lithographed in Gujaráti composition. ય ya and ષ *sa* have not hitherto been typographed. As the literature of Gujarát improves, it will be nesessary to render the Gujaráti alphabet equivalent to the Bálbodh. Attempts at a correct orthography are useless without adopting this measure. Lithography has already advanced to this point. It remains for typography to do the same.

BÁLBODH AND GUJARÁTI ALPHABETS.

Bálbodh.	Gujaráti.	Corresponding nglish vowels.	Vowels. Power in English Letters.	Represented by Roman letters in this work.
अ	અ	a or u	1. a short as in *America*. 2. u as in f*u*n.	a, ă *
आ	આ	a	1. a long as in f*a*rce. 2. broad as in w*a*rm	á, à
इ	ઇ	e or i	1. e short as in d*e*ceive. 2. i short as in ch*i*p	i, ĭ
ई		e or ee	e long as in adh*e*re, or ee as in m*ee*t.	í
उ	ઉ	u or oo	u short as in f*u*ll, or oo as in g*oo*d.	u
ऊ		u or oo	u long as in r*u*de, or oo as in f*oo*d.	ú
ऋ			See Remarks on Pronunciation.	ru
ॠ			"	rú
ऌ			"	lu
ॡ			"	lú
ए	એ	a	1. a long as in n*a*me. 2. a short as in Th*a*mes.	é, e
ऐ	ઐ	i or ie	nearly i as in ice or ie as in die.	ai
ओ	ઓ	o	1. o long as in b*o*ne. 2. o short as in pron*o*unce.	o
औ	ઔ	ou	nearly ou as in h*ou*se.	a u
ं	ં		a nasal sound (see Remarks on Pronunciation).	ng ṇ n m
ः			a final aspirate (see Remarks on Pronunciation).	

* Let the reader carefully observe the power of the Roman letter, lest he should be deceived by the analogy of sounds of the English vowels.

The Roman letters, let him observe, nearly correspond in power to those used on the continent of Europe.

CONSONANTS.

Class.	Bálbodh.	Gujaráti.	In English Letters.	Represented by Roman Letters.
Gutturals.	क	ક	ka *	k
	ख	ખ	kha	kh
	ग	ગ	ga	g
	घ	ઘ	gha	gh
	ङ	†	nga	ng
Palatals.	च	ચ	cha	ch
	छ	છ	chha	cha
	ज	જ	ja or za	j or z
	झ	ઝ	jha	jh
	ञ	‡	nya	n
Cerebrals.	ट	ટ	ta	ṭ
	ठ	ઠ	tha	ṭh
	ड	ડ	da	ḍ
	ढ	ઢ	dha	ḍh
	ण ण	ણ	gna	ṇ
Dentals	त	ત	ta	t
	थ	થ	tha	th
	द	દ	da	d
	ध	ધ	dha	dh
	न	ન	na	n

* Read *a* with the short sound as belonging to the vowel અ.

Thus read ka as ca in Americ*a*, ga as in Malag*a*, and so on with all the consonants.

† Represented by the Anusvara or by the dental ન.

‡ Represented by the Anusvara or by the dental ન.

CONSONANTS.—Continued.

Class.	Bálbodh.	Gujaráti.	Name in English Letters.	Represented by Roman Letters in this work.
Labials.	प	પ	pa	p
	फ	ફ	pha	ph
	ब	બ	ba	b
	भ भ	ભ	bha	bh
	म	મ	ma	m
Miscellaneous.	य	ય	ya	y
	र	ર	ra	r
	ल	લ	la	l
	व	વ	vo	v
	श श	શ	sha	ṣ
	ष	*	sha	sh
	स	શ સ	sa	s
	ह	હ	ha	h
	ळ	†	la	l
Compounds.	क्ष	‡	ksha	ksh
	ज्ञ	‖	dnya	dny

* This is occasionally represented by ખ, and by શ.

† This is represented by ળ.

‡ This is represented frequently by ખ, or ખ શ.

‖ Sometimes represented by ગ્ન and ન.

Remarks on pronunciation of the letters.

1. VOWELS.

B. G. R.
अ अ અ અ a ă. This vowel sound is inherent in every consonant sounded singly. It is met with in its appropriate form generally as an initial either of a word or of a syllable.

1. When it is a negative particle * or when it is followed by હ, or by any letter of the cerebral class and occasionally by ર, or when the consonant in which it inheres, is itself a particle †, or in *whatever case it may be considered either alone or as inherent in the consonant to constitute a syllable*, it has the short sound of *a*, as we find it expressed in a-going, a-head, a-way, &c. when sounded quickly as in conversation, or of the French *e* in the article *Le*.

2. When followed by any one of the vowels આ ઈ ઉ ઔ ઐ, the above sound is somewhat modified according to the particular vowel so as to approach, when blended with either of those vowels, to a diphthong.

3. When it is followed by any consonant not mentioned above into which it is resolvable in the same syllable, or when it is headed by a nasal that is not followed by a cerebral, or *when in any case it may be considered as an element of a syllable*, it has the short sound of *u* in cupboard. This sound is exceedingly frequent in pure Gujaráti words, especially in verbal roots.

---

* અ is a negative affix in Sanscrit words.

† E. G. કુ is a Gujaráti affix signifying bad.

This vowel is used in the Gujaráti for ય, but it is utterly inadequate to represent it and its discontinuation is desirable.

There are other forms of this letter but not in type. They are used chiefly by Váṇiyas.

E. G. અશુધ asúdh, impure ; અંગ ăngg, body.

B. G. R.
आ आ આ આ a á. Is not correctly represented by the English *a*, being sounded less broadly than it, like the French *a* in *La*. Its length however depends somewhat on the presence or absence of accent.*

2. When followed by a final વ, especially when this is followed by a labial, or headed by an anúsvara, it has frequently a broader sound than the above, approaching to the circumflexed â.

3. When it is followed by the vowels ઇ ઉ એ, or by the semivowel ય, it undergoes some modification for the sake of euphony, and nearly coalesces with the succeeding letter so as to form a diphthong.

The peculiar modification can only be attained from a correct speaker. There are other forms of this letter, corresponding to those of અ.

E. G. આપો àpo, give ચામડું, chámaḍúng, leather.

B. G. R.
इ ઇ i ĭ. Has the short sound of e in *de*cay. In several positions, especially when it is followed by a double consonant, or headed by a nasal not followed by a cerebral, it has the short sound of *i* in cinder. Popular use however is not uniform.

E. G. શીશો ṣiso, bottle ; ચીંતા chĭntá, care.

---

* Let it be observed that accent in Gujaráti does not involve so great a stress as is laid on syllables in English.

B. G. R.
ई ઈ i í. Is the above lengthened, as *e* in adhere, or *ea* in s*ea*red.

The reader in Gujaráti can decide only by the ear as to the length of the ઈ, as there is no distinction in the character.

E. G. ईश्वर ísvar, God; कवी kăví poet.

B. G. G.
ए એ é e. Is the English *a* as in n*a*me, perhaps somewhat less broad and full. It is in some few words, especially monosyllables, somewhat clipped in pronunciation; as *a* in Thames.

E. G. સેવક sévak, servant; જેમ jem, as.

B. G. R.
ऐ ઐ ai. Is a diphthongal sound. It is nearly like the English *i* in ice, or *is* in isle, or *ie* in die. This diphthong does not consist of આ & ઈ, in which case it would be like the ai in *ai*sle, but of અ & ઈ. The Scotch accent in the pronunciation of g*ui*le, find, &c. gives the force of this vowel; also the German *ei*. When the vowels અ & ઈ meet in Gujaráti composition they are sounded as this vowel, with the exception that the latter sound is more lengthened. This vowel is therefore seldom used.

E. G. પૈ pai, a pie; પૈસો paiso, a pice.

B. G. R.
ओ ઓ o. Is reputed a diphthong, but is questionable as such. It has the long sound of o in bone, and when the accent is not in it, it has the short sound of o in p*ro*nounce. It never has the short sound of o in hot, lot, &c. which is uncongenial to the language, and which cannot be presented nearer than by the vowel આ.

E. G. ઓશડ osaḍ, medicine; જો jo, if.

B. G. R.
औ ઔ au. Is a diphthong composed of અ & ઉ.

It is not so full a sound nor so mouthed (so to speak) as the English ou or ow, but the organs are more compressed in its articulation; ou in the verb h*ou*se approaches the sound. If pronounced with the Scotch accent, it more nearly corresponds. It is said to be represented properly by the German au; અ & ઉ when they meet are sounded as this diphthong with the exception that the latter sound is more lengthened. This vowel is therefore of unfrequent use.

E. G. કૌસ kauṣ, parenthesis.

B. G. R.
ં ં ng. (final.) Is called in Sanscrit anusvara, and in Gujaráti, mindu, a point. It is the symbol of a nasal sound, which is attachable to any of the vowels when expressed, or the અ unexpressed but inherent in the consonant. This sound cannot well be represented by English letters. When heading a vowel not followed by a consonant, it is approached by the mp in *aide de camp* as generally sounded, or the n in the French *bon*. It is rather softer than the ng in sang. Its pronunciation is not uniformly observed, nor when observed is it with uniform distinctness. The anusvara is also a representative of the five nasal consonants. (See Consonants, page).

E. G. અં ăng, આં áng, ઉં ung, ઔં ong, &c. &c.

B.
: Is called visurg. It is a final aspirate, corresponding in sound to a soft h. It may be expressed in Gujaráti by હ. It is occasionally changed into an ર.

E. G. અંત:કરણ is in Gujaráti written and pronounced અંતરકરણ. It may be represented by ah in Roman letters.

2. CONSONANTS.

Obs. 1. Although words are frequently compounded by prepositions, &c. and are written as one word, they are to be considered for the purposes of pronunciation as perfectly independent.

E. G. માંણુશમાંથી consists of માંણુશ and માં and થી, and their respective finals are શ. આં. થી.

When initials and finals are treated of, this principle is to be remembered.

Obs. 2. 1. Every consonant sounded individually has in it the sound of the vowel અ expressed subsequently to the consonantal sounds.

2. If the consonant be blended with another consonant, (see the second Table) this vowel is not sounded.

3. If the consonant be final and single, this vowel is not sounded.

Exception.—It is sounded slightly after a compound consonant, of which the first element is not sibilant, or after a final વ and final ય. Words containing such elements are of Sanscrit origin.

Obs. 3. When the vowel sound અ inherent in the nasal consonants, is designed to be dropped, it is represented by the anuswara. Strictly speaking, *the power of this point when followed by a classed consonant in the same word, is that of the nasal of the class to which that consonant belongs.* Custom, however, is not exactly conformable to this principle.

When followed by an unclassed consonant, its power approaches as nearly as possible to that of such consonant; (see the third Table) i. e. the same organs are used in the pronunciation of both.

Obs. 4. The aspirate letters of each class are articulated by *breathing out* their respective consonants. No interval of time should elapse between the articulation of the consonant and its aspirate, nor should any new configuration of the organs take place. *The sound is to be emitted at once, so as to form an unbroken articulation, as of an individual letter.*

GUTTURALS.

B. G. R.
क ક ka. Has the sound of the English k, or of the hard c; as in kernel, caprice, &c.

E. G. કાપ káp, cut; બીહીક bíhík, fear.

B. G. R.
ख ખ kha. Is the above aspirated (see Obs. 4).

It is used occasionally, as well as the preceding for the Persian ق, and is sounded accordingly by the learned in that language but not by the common people.

E. G. આખો ákho, whole; માખી mákhí, fly.

B. G. R.
ग ગ ga. Is the English hard g, as in gun.

This letter is used to represent غ in Persian words and is sounded by the learned accordingly.

E. G. ગોળ gól, round; મગર măgar, alligator.

B. G. R.
घ ઘ gha. Is the above aspirated.

E. G. વાઘ vágh, tiger; ઘાસ ghás, grass.

B. G. R.
ङ ઙ nga. This is the nasal of the class and therefore guttural; it is pronounced nearly as ng in wrung.

E. G. રંગારો rănggáro, painter; પંખો păngkho, fan.

PALATALS.

B. G. R.
च ચ cha. Is pronounced as ch in church. It has not two

sounds as in Maráthi, but is sounded more or less as a sharp by different speakers.

E. G. ચોખો chokho, pure; લાંચ lánch, bribe.

B. G. R.
छ છ chha. Is its aspirate.

E. G. છોકરો chokaro, boy; છેક chék, utterly.

B. G. R.
ज જ ja. Is the English *j* pronounced more or less softly by different speakers. In pure Gujaráti words it has this sound alone, but it is used for the Persian ز and is then sounded like the English z. e. g. નિમાજ nímáz, religious service. This sound, however, is uncommon where there is no Persian or Hindustánl spoken.

E. G. જાણ jáṇ, know; સાજો sájo, sane, sound.

B. G. R.
झ ઝ jha. Is its aspirate; another Gujaráti form is ઝ

E. G. ઝાડ jhád, tree; ઝુલ jhúl, swing.

B. G. R.
ञ ઞ ñ. Is the nasal of this class. It is pronounced on the palate and is softer than the guttural. It sounds like a nasal y, the n being made very nasal, by the suppression of the breath in the nostrils.

E. G. સાંચો sáñcho, machine; પાંજરૂં páñjarúng, cage.

Cerebrals.

The cerebrals (so called from the fact that they when sounded seem to proceed from the cerebrum), are articulated by turning the tip of the tongue back and applying it to the palate. A hollow consonant-sound is thereby produced,—unknown in the

English alphabet, so that there are no perfect representatives of this class.

B. G. R.
ट ટ ṭa. This letter differs from the English t, in that it is not like it pronounced on the osseous part of the gums near the teeth, but above it with the tongue turned back towards the palate according to the nature of the class.

E. G. ટટ્ટુ ṭaṭú, a poney; ટળવું ṭălavúng, to move away.

B. G. R.
ठ ઠ ṭha. Is the aspirate of the above.

E. G. માઠો màṭho, bad; સાઠ sáṭh, sixty.

B. G R.
ड ડ ḍa. Differs from the English d, in the way peculiar to the class. It has two sounds. When it is initial or when it follows the point, it is a distinct d as above described. In other position it is between the above d, and an r; this sound being produced by the quick withdrawment of the tongue from the position requisite for the pronunciation of the former. As a general rule, its greater or less distinctness depends on the vowel which precedes it.

E. G. ડામર ḍámar, pitch; બેચડ Béchaḍ, (name); ગાડી gáḍí, carriage.

B. G. R.
ढ ઢ ḍha. Is the aspirate of the above, and is always sounded with great force.

E G. ઢાલ ḍhál, shield; ઢંઢેરો ḍhăndhéro, instrument of music.

B. G. R.
ण ण ણ ṇa. Is the nasal of the class pronounced, somewhat like the French gne in Charlemagne.

E. G. પ્રમાણે pramáṇé, like to; નિશાણી nisáṇi, sign.

Dentals.

The dentals do not correspond to the English dentals. Those are sounded by placing the tongue on the osseous gum near the teeth, whereas the Gujaráti are sounded by the tongue placed between the teeth, not protruding but resting on the root of the upper row.

B. G. R.
त ત ta. Is the English t, pronounced as above; t in tube, nearly approaches to it.

E. G. મેતા méto, clerk; સાત sát, seven.

B. G. R.
थ થ tha. Is the aspirate of the above.

E. G. હાથ háth, hand; જથો jathó, troop.

B. G. R.
द દ da. Is the English d, pronounced as above.

The d in dupe nearly approaches to it.

E. G. દાંત dánt, tooth; સાદો sádo, plain.

B. G. R.
ध ધ dha. Is the aspirate of the above.

E. G. કીધેલો kídhélo, done; ઊધાર údhár, loan.

B. G. R.
न ન na. Is the nasal of the class nearly approaching the English n. e. g. નાળીએર nálíér, cocoanut; છાનો chàno, secret.

Labials.

B. G. R.
प પ pa. Is the English p.

E. G. પોથી pothi, book; સાપ sáp, snake.

B. G. R.
फ ફ pha. Is the above aspirated.

E. G. ફળ phăl, fruit; ફુલ phul, flower.

Pársís sound it like f; it may be right to sound it so, when representing the Persian, but this sound is not congenial to Gujaráti and is to be considered as impure.

B. G. R.
ब બ ba. Is the English b.

E. G. બમણો bămaṇo, double ; લાંબો làmbo, long.

B. G. R.
भ भ ભ bha. Is the aspirate of the above.

E. G. ભોજન bhojan, meal ; ભો bho, fear.

B. G. R.
म મ ma. Is the English m, it is also the nasal of its class, and is represented by the anusvara.

E. G. માર már, beat ; નામ nàm, name.

Individual Consonants.

B. G. R.
य ય ya. Has the power of the English y.

It is a palatal and semi-vowel when final. It is not yet adopted in Gujaráti composition, although the recurrence of the sound in every past tense of a verb, renders its use indispensable to correct orthography. This letter occurring in Sanscrit words, is often corrupted in Gujaráti into j. e. g. मर्यादा is corrupted into મરજાદા respect. यात्रा into જાતરા pilgrimage.

E. G. માયા máyá, delusion ; કન્યા kănyá, virgin.

B. G. R.
र ર ra. Has the power of the English r, it is sometimes a semi-vowel being resolvable into the following consonant. This power is signified in Balbodh by inserting it in a shortened form, over the consonant into whose sound it resolves: This distinction cannot be made in Gujaráti.

E. G. રડ raḍ, weep; ઓરડી ordi, room.

B. G. R
ल લ la. Is a dental, sounded *on*, not *between*, the teeth.

E. G. લે lé, take; શાલો sálo, brother-in-law.

B. G. R.
व વ va. Is a dento-labial; it is not the exact equivalent of either v or w. It is sounded by the teeth without their compressing the lip as done in sounding v, and also by the lips in a more contracted form than is necessary to articulate w. It is sounded with the teeth, the under lip being drawn in, upon the under teeth, but not made to meet the upper teeth. The uneducated approximate the sound to w, and the educated to v. When initial, it more nearly approaches to u; and when final, to a w.

E. G. પાવ páv, quarter; શવલો săvalo, right, in order.

B. G. R.
श श્ર શ ṣa. Is a sibilant proceeding from the palate; it is articulated by applying the lip of the tongue to the forepart of the palate. It approaches to the English sh, but is not so sibyllant.

E. G. શબ્દ ṣăbda, word; શંસાર ṣănsár, world.

B. R.
ष ṣha. Is a cerebral; it has the power of the English *sh* in shock, if sounded high on the palate softly. In Gujaráti the sound is corrupted into that of શ. e. g. ભાશા, and this character is accordingly used. It is sometimes also corrupted into ખ.

B. G. R.
स સ શ sa. Is a dental. It has the power of the English s. The form most commonly in Gujaráti use is શ; સ is adopted by the Bramins. e. g. સોએ soé, needle; સાધુ sádhú, saint.

B. G. B.
ह હ ha. Is an aspirate. It may be expressed by the English h, but is more of a guttural character. It is represented

at the end of a word in Balbodh composition by the two points.

E. G. હીરો híro, diamond; હોજો hójo, water-drawer.

B. R.
ळ la. Is a cerebral l, sounded further back in the palate than the other cerebrals. There is a lythographed Gujaráti form but it is generally represented by લ.

E. G. બોલવું bolavung, to dip.

B. R.
क्ष ksha. Is a compound in sound, and it is supposed in form of क्ष. In Gujaráti few, save the learned, pronounce it. It is generally corrupted into ખ or ખશ.

E. G. क्षत्री is corrupted into ખતરી. A student should not adopt such corruptions.

B. R.
ज्ञ dnya. Is never met with, but in Sanscrit words.

Vowels coalescent with Consonants.

It has been seen that every consonant sounded by itself has in it the sound of the vowel અ. It becomes necessary to represent consonants in a state of immediate combination with other vowel sounds save that of અ. To accomplish this, an imperfect form of the vowel is employed, which coalesces with the consonant. The consonant then drops its own inherent vowel sound, and adopts the sound of the vowel thus subjoined.*

The vowel as represented in the alphabet is in its isolate form. This may be called its perfect form. *In this form it is either initial, or follows a vowel either expressed or inherent in the*

* Whether this theory exactly corresponds to fact or not, it presents perhaps the most satisfactory elucidation to the student.

consonant. As represented below, it is in its coalescent form. This may be called its imperfect form. *This form is never employed save when following a consonant which drops its own vowel sound.*

Bálbodh Isolate and Coalescent Vowels.

आ	इ	ई	उ	ऊ	ऋ	ए	ऐ	ओ	औ
ा	ि	ी	ु	ू	ृ	े	ै	ो	ौ

Gujaráti Isolate and Coalescent Vowels.

આ	ઈ	ઊ	એ	ઐ	ઓ	ઔ
ા	ી	ૂ	ે	ૈ	ો	ૌ

Bálbodh Consonant क with Coalescent Vowels.

क का कि की कु कू के कै को कौ

And so on throughout the Alphabot.

GUJARATI ALPHABET WITH COALESCENT VOWELS.*

TABLE 1.

ká	કા	kí	કી	ku†	કુ	ké	કે	kai	કૈ	ko	કો	kau	કૌ
khá	ખા	khí	ખી	khu	ખુ	khé	ખે	khai	ખૈ	kho	ખો	khau	ખૌ
gá	ગા	gí	ગી	gu	ગુ	gé	ગે	gai	ગૈ	go	ગો	gau	ગૌ
ghá	ઘા	ghí	ઘી	ghu	ઘુ	ghé	ઘે	ghai	ઘૈ	gho	ઘો	ghau	ઘૌ
chá	ચા	chí	ચી	chu	ચુ	ché	ચે	chai	ચૈ	cho	ચો	chau	ચૌ
chhá	છા	chhí	છી	chhu	છુ	chhé	છે	chhai	છૈ	chho	છો	chhau	છૌ

* The mastering of the above table will render the task of reading easy. Let the reader refer to the alphabet for the correct sound of the Roman letters.

† u either with or without an accent.

já	જા	jí	જી	ju	જુ	jè	જે	jai	જૈ	jo	જો	jau	જૌ
jhá	ઝા	jhí	ઝી	jhu	ઝુ	jhè	ઝે	jhai	ઝૈ	jho	ઝો	jhau	ઝૌ
ṭá	ટા	ṭí	ટી	ṭu	ટુ	ṭé	ટે	ṭai	ટૈ	ṭo	ટો	ṭau	ટૌ
ṭhá	ઠા	ṭhí	ઠી	ṭhu	ઠુ	ṭhé	ઠે	ṭhai	ઠૈ	ṭho	ઠો	ṭhau	ઠૌ
ḍá	ડા	ḍí	ડી	ḍu	ડુ	ḍé	ડે	ḍai	ડૈ	ḍo	ડો	ḍau	ડૌ
ḍhá	ઢા	ḍhí	ઢી	ḍhu	ઢુ	ḍhé	ઢે	ḍhai	ઢૈ	ḍho	ઢો	ḍhau	ઢૌ
ṇá	ણા	ṇí	ણી	ṇu	ણુ	ṇé	ણે	ṇai	ણૈ	ṇo	ણો	ṇau	ણૌ
tá	તા	tí	તી	tu	તુ	té	તે	tai	તૈ	to	તો	tau	તૌ
thá	થા	thí	થી	thu	થુ	thé	થે	thai	થૈ	tho	થો	thau	થૌ
dá	દા	dí	દી	du	દુ	dé	દે	dai	દૈ	do	દો	dau	દૌ
dhá	ધા	dhí	ધી	dhu	ધુ	dhé	ધે	dhai	ધૈ	dho	ધો	dhau	ધૌ
ná	ના	ní	ની	nu	નુ	né	ને	nai	નૈ	no	નો	nau	નૌ
pá	પા	pí	પી	pu	પુ	pé	પે	pai	પૈ	po	પો	pau	પૌ
phá	ફા	phí	ફી	phu	ફુ	phé	ફે	phai	ફૈ	pho	ફો	phau	ફૌ
bá	બા	bí	બી	bu	બુ	bé	બે	bai	બૈ	bo	બો	bau	બૌ
bhá	ભા	bhí	ભી	bhu	ભુ	bhé	ભે	bhai	ભૈ	bho	ભો	bhau	ભૌ
má	મા	mí	મી	mu	મુ	mé	મે	mai	મૈ	mo	મો	mau	મૌ
yá	યા	yí	યી	yu	યુ	yé	યે	yai	યૈ	yo	યો	yau	યૌ
rá	રા	rí	રી	ru	રુ	ré	રે	rai	રૈ	ro	રો	rau	રૌ
lá	લા	lí	લી	lu	લુ	lé	લે	lai	લૈ	lo	લો	lau	લૌ
vá	વા	ví	વી	vu	વુ	vé	વે	vai	વૈ	vo	વો	vau	વૌ
ṣá	શા	ṣí	શી	ṣu	શુ	ṣé	શે	ṣai	શૈ	ṣo	શો	ṣau	શૌ
sá	સા	sí	સી	su	સુ	sé	સે	sai	સૈ	so	સો	sau	સૌ
há	હા	hí	હી	hu	હુ	hé	હે	hai	હૈ	ho	હો	hau	હૌ

Consonants coalescing with Consonants.

When consonants are blended in sound together, without the intervention of the inherent અ, they are blended likewise in form and become compound letters, called in Gujaráti जोडअक्षरो jodă-ksharo. The rule generally observed from blending them, is as follows:—The first part of the former whether one or more, is joined to the last part or to the whole of the final letter. A symbol of the letter ર called réph, is placed frequently over the letter when it is a semivowel running into the succeeding consonant as, in the word सर्व sarva, all. Bálbodh employs these compounded consonants, and a few are occasionally found in the Gujaráti, but they are not in general use. Below is a table of those commonly used in Balbodh.

Table illustrative of the power of the Anusvara before classed consonants.

TABLE 3.

Gut.	*Palat.*	*Cere.*	*Den.*	*Labi.*
Power of ङ	Power of ञ	Power of ण	Power of न	Power of म
શાંકલ	સાંચો	ઈંડાં	દાંત	ચાંપો
sángkal	saṅcho	iṇdáng	dánt	chámpo
chain.	machine.	eggs.	tooth.	squeeze.

Observe. The force of the Anusvara is equivalent to the nasal of the class to which the consonant which follows it belongs. Its force becomes modified when preceding the unclassed letters, inasmuch as it is pronounced with the same organs as are employed in sounding the respective consonant. e. g. શ is a sibilant dental, the Anusvara therefore will approach the sound of dental ન, and so on with the rest.

GUJARÁTI DOUBLE CONSONANTS.

ક્ય Kya	ક્ર Kra	કૃ Krú	ક્સ Ksa	ખ્ર Khra	ગ્ગ gga	ગ્દ gda	ગ્ધ gdha
ગ્ન gna	ગ્મ gma	ગ્ય gya	ગ્ર gra	ઘ્ય ghya	ગૃ grú	ગ્લ gla	ગ્વ gva
ચ્ચ chcha	ચ્છ chha	ચ્ય chya	જ્જ jja	જ્ય jya	ડ્ર dra	ટ્ટ ṭṭa	ટ્ઠ ṭṭha
ટ્ય ṭya	ડ્ય ḍya	ઢ્ય ḍhya	ણ્ણ ṇṇa	ણ્હ ṇha	ણ્ય ṇya	ણ્મ ṇma	ત્ત tta
ત્થ ttha	ત્પ tpa	ત્વ tva	પ્ત pta	ત્મ tma	ત્મ્ય tmya	તૃ trú	ત્ર tra
ત્ન tna	થ્ય thya	દ્વ dva	દૃ drú	દ્ય dya	ધ્ય dhya	ધ્વ dhva	ધ્ર dhra
ન્ન nna	ન્ય nya	ન્હ nha	ન્વ nva	ન્દ nda	ન્પ npa	ન્મ nma	પ્ર pra
ફ્ર phra	બ્ર bra	વ્ય vya	ભ્ય bhya	મ્મ mma	મ્પ mpa	મ્ય mya	મ્હ mha
લ્લ lla	લ્હ્ય lhaya	લ્ય lya	લ્મ lma	લ્ગ lga	લ્હ lha	લ્પ lpa	લ્ફ lpha
ષ્ટ shṭa	ષ્ટ્ર shṭra	વ્વ vva	વ્હ vha	વૃ vrú	શ્ર shra	સ્વ sva	શ્ચ shch
સ્સ ssa	સ્ય sya	સ્મ sma	ષ્ફ shph	શ્વ shva	ષ્ય shya	સ્ત્ર stra	સ્પ spa
સ્ત્વ stva	સ્ફ sph	સ્ન sna	સ્મ sma	સ્ય sya	સ્ત sta	હ્ય hya	લ્લ્ય llya

Observe. The representation of the point in Roman letters is the same as that of the nasals of the respective classes. This rule will be observed throdghout this work.

TABLE 4. (Exercises.)

રાજા	rája	king	ભાઈ	bhái	brother
પરમેશ્વર	paramésvar	God	મરણ	mărăṇ	death
ભીત	bhít	wall	વાડી	váḍí	garden
ચોપડી	chopaḍí	book	પાંનું	pànnúng	leaf
લુઘડું	lúghaḍúng	cloth	ખુરસી	khúrsi	chair
વીચાર	víchár	thought	કલમ	kălăm	pen
ભાગ	bhág	share	રૂપીઓ	rupío	rupee
ફુલ	phúl	flower	ચમચો	chămcho	spoon
પાણી	páṇí	water	કાગલ	kágal	paper
પથર	păthar	stone	રેસમ	rèsăm	silk
ઘાશ	ghás̩	grass	રસી	răsi	string
માણુશ	màṇas	man	પેઆલું	péálúng	cup
બેહેન	béhén	sister	મીઠું	miṭhúng	salt
ગેટું	géṭúng	sheep	દુધ	dúdh	milk
બકરી	băkari	goat	લાકડું	lákaḍúng	wood
દરવાજો	darvájo	door	બાલક	bálak	infant
નદી	nădí	river	સીરકો	sírko	vinegar
દીકરો	díkaro	son	છડી	chhaḍi	cane
કુઓ	kúo	well	પાગડી	págaḍi	turban
અનાજ	anáj	corn	ટોપી	ṭopí	cap
ખાવાનું	khávánúng	food	જોડો	joḍo	shoe
શીસી	s̩ísí	phial	હાડકું	háḍkúng	bone

ભાગલ	bhágal	gate	લોક	lok	people
કામડી	kàmaḍí	bamboo	વાત	vát	word
ચામડું	chàmaḍúng	leather	ઘુંટણ	ghúnṭaṇ	knee
નખ	năkh	nail	સીપાઈ	sipái	soldier
હાથ	háth	hand	ડકાલ	ḍakál	famine
આંખ	ángkh	eye	વરશ	vărăṣ	year
નીમાલા	nimálá	hair	મહીનો	mahíno	month
હીસાબ	hísáb	account	અઠવાડીઉં	aṭhváḍíúng	week

(For further lessons on reading see Exercises.)

Observe. As Gujaráti does not distinguish between the long and short vowels, the Roman í and ú, as given in this work, may be either short or long.

II. ETYMOLOGY.

1st. Part.

Components of the Language.

The Gujaráti language, if analyzed as the English, may be said to comprise the Substantive, the Adjective, the Pronoun, the Verb, the Preposition, the Conjunction, the Adverb (including particles), and the Interjection, to which may be added the Article. * The four first parts of speech are in a limited degree declinable, the fifth, the preposition, is so in one instance only, and the four last are indeclinable.

---

* It may be contended by some conversant with the language, that there is no Article. The Author presumes to say there is. He means by "Article" a particle whose office it is to define in a certain way, and which cannot, on acount of its own peculiar power, be resolved into any other part of speech. This particle is the numeral એક. It neither corresponds to the English indefinite article nor to the definite, but is still an Article. It resigns occasionally its numerical meaning and defines or more correctly individualizes. Its peculiar force will be evinced by a comparison with the English indefinite.

1. It widely differs from this article in one respect ;—The English *distributes* or signifies *any* individual of a whole class, as Ex. a man has two feet, i. e. any and every man. The Gujaráti article does not distribute in any way. The distribution is involved in the substantive itself without any qualifying particle. The Gujaráti language makes the substantive to represent the whole class and predicates of that class as thus represented. It does not, as the English,

Substantive.

Number.

1. Substantives have two numbers, the Singular and Plural.

2. All Substantives, significative of objects which may be more

---

choose an indefinite individual of the class and make its predications of it. What it predicates it predicates of the whole as comprehended in the substantive.

2. The English article in some cases *individualizes or expresses an individual of a class as present in the matter of individuality to the conception of the speaker*: as, yesterday *a* gentleman came to my house. Here thereis no definition of the object, neither is there a distribution of it, but there is an individualization of a member of a class. This is the exact power of the Gujaráti particle. Whenever used as an article, which it is very frequently, it is intended to represent the idea, not of an individual as distinguished numerically from two or three or more, nor of an individual as distinguished in quality from others of the class, *but of an individual present to the conception as an individual,* as a certain one which it is in no way designed to define, but which is assuredly the object of actual conception to the mind of the speaker as an individual. In no wise could such a conception be conveyed without the use of the એકુ. Its omission would induce a different idea. The use of the substantive without the article in most cases involves some specific individual, or marks out the whole class. There arises from the above principles the apparent anomaly that this article may be in most cases rendered in English by "a certain," whilst કોઈએકુ, (literally any one,) is often the rendering of "a," being the more indefinite of the twain. Let it then be remembered that the power of એકુ as an article is uniform: it does not define as to quality or circumstance in the fact of numerical unity *but in the simple fact of individuality* relatively to the conception of the mind. (See remarks on the demonstrative pronouns), and on the pronoun કોઈએકુ.

than one in nature, *may*, if necessary, assume a plural form irrespectively of termination.

3. All Substantives that denote objects having an essential unity, do not of course take the plural form.

4. Substantives denoting objects, having essential plurality, do not take a plural form.* Such are those which denote species of grain, spice, &c. &c.

5. Substantives qualified by Adjectives, &c. in the plural form, or by numerals, do not necessarily take the full plural form, but simply the oblique one (See Substantive). The practice of the more correct speakers is, however, more favourable to the expression of the plural in case of plurality than its suppression. Euphony is the sole standard of authority for the use or disuse of the form. Euphony should be sacrificed to perspecuity, especially in composition.

Case. †

Substantives have cases to denote their relations to each other or to other parts of speech. Three cases exist in this language

---

* There are apparent exceptions to this. લોક people takes the plural form લોકો. The reason is that the several objects are viewed as an aggregate one, which itself may be multiplied.

† The word "case" in its original application, signified an inflected form of the substantive itself, by which its different relations to other parts of speech were indicated. In this strict sense there is but one case in the Gujaráti Substantive, viz. the vocative, and even this is not always a case, being very frequently of the same form as the nominative, i. e. as the substantive itself. The word case is here used in its widest signification in the grammatical relationship of a substantive, whether indicated by an inflexion or a preposition, or by neither as in the accusative case. Without referring substantives to certain cases, we can make no grammatical analysis of sentences: I have therefore declined the

without prepositions. These are the Nominative, the Vocative, and Accusative.* The rest are formed by post-fixing of prepositions.† Hence there are literally as many cases as there are generic prepositions, which may be post fixed to the substantive. The chief prepositional cases are as follows: 1. The case formed by the post-fix of the declinable preposition નો of.‡ 2. by the

---

Noun in six cases. It is not to be considered that these are the only cases. The prepositional cases have been chosen, because expressive of the most frequent and important relations. It is evident that the substantive might be declined by medium of all the prepositions which specifically differ in their signification.

* The Student must not attend to the etymology of the word but to its grammatical power, which is the same as that of the English preposition. It is by some called a post-position, but this is an uncouth word, and adapted to prevent the student from recognizing its true nature.

† The accusatve or objective case, which, in all classes of substantives, retains the same form as the nominative, simply denotes objectiveness of the substantive relatively to the verb. This case consequently can only be used when the object signified by the substantive is considered as unaffected by the action signified by the verb. It expresses only the relation of the *substantive* to the *verb*, and not the relation of the object expressed by the substantive to the action expressed by the verb. To express this latter is the province of the dative alone. This language indicates all relations of objects by prepositions. The accusative has no prepositions, and hence no relation of objects is indicated by it. In the phrase મે લાકડી મારી the literal translation is, I struck a stick; but as the substantive is in the accusative, the meaning is, that the stick was the vehicle of the action strike, and *not* the object of the action. In this example the object *stick* may be said to be governed by the verb, but only in a grammatical sense, since the action of the verb does not pass over to the object.

‡ Genitive expresses the general relationship of inherence or connection with any thing in the sense of property. The preposition is declined as an adjective of the same termination (see Preposition). It is post-fixed to the sub-

post-fix of ને to: this may be called the Dative* or the cases

---

stantive significative of the subject, i. e. of the possessor and agrees in gender and number with the following substantive, which signifies the object of possession, i. e. the thing possessed. Hence it corresponds in position and character to the Saxon post-fix 's. Ex. The king's horse.

The more important specific relations may be classed as follows :

1. of property	e. g.	છોકરાની ચોપડી	the boy's book.
2. of material	„	રૂપાનો ચમચો	a silver spoon (of silver a spoon).
3. of subjectiveness	„	ઈશ્વરનો સ્વભાવ	nature of God.
4. of objectiveness	„	ઈશ્વરનો વીચાર	thought of (respecting) God.
5. of source or origin	„	વીલાએતનાં લુગડાં	of England the cloths, i. e. from England.

* *This case expresses finality or the issue of the action of the verb. It does this invariably and this alone.*

Whenever the object signified by the substantive is to be represented as effected in the order of nature by the action of the verb, this case is employed. It has the sign ને to, expressing finality. The English language employs this case to express finality only where there is *something* intermediate, as I gave the money *to* the boy. But the Gujaráti language employs this case whether there be any thing intermediate or not. Ex. 1. મે છોકરાને રૂપીઓ આપો, I gave a rupee to the boy. Here it is as in English—there is something intermediate. Ex. 2. મે છોકરાને મારો, I beat *to* the boy. Here it differs from the English. There is nothing intermediate. In both these examples, however, the dative possesses the same power. It sustains the transitiveness of the action of the verb. It likewise occurs that, when the verb governs two objects, the one of which is intermediate relatively to the other, yet being both relatively to the verb final; in other words, objects to both of which the action of the verb passes over, are both put in the dative case, as તેણે છોકરાને વેપારીને વેચાતા આપો he sold *to* the boy *to* the merchant.

Here each dative fulfils the same purpose. It is the subject of, or so to speak, the recipient of the action of the verb. If the verb denote action that is transitive, the substantive must be put in the dative case to signify that it is the object which sustains the transition. That action passes first to the one, and thence to

denoting the being affected by some transitive action. 3. The

---

the other; both are alike final relatively to the verb, and therefore both are put in the dative.

This law of the language may present at first some difficulty to the student. A brief illustration from the English language will remove it. The English verb generally gives the noun in the objective case, yet if we resolve the verb into its abstract action, and another verb significant of transitiveness, it becomes imperative to use the dative case. Ex. "I beat the boy," may be resolved into "I gave a beating to the boy." 2. "I injured the man," may be resolved into "I did an injury *to* the man." The mode of thought involved in these expressions is the *exact* mode of thought developed in the use of Gujaráti verbs governing the dative.

The verbs in Latin which govern a dative case, likewise illustrate the government of the Gujaráti verbs.

It must be acknowledged that there is much diversity in the respective uses of the dative and accusative cases. They are frequently used interchangeably. The reason is obvious. Finality of object is not an idea which present itself alike to all minds, or to the same mind under all circumstances, and hence the less discriminating speaker uses the accusative which is the readier form Careless speakers will be found to use the accusative, when the generally correct speaker uses the dative. The English student should avoid looseness of speech in this respect. The following may be adopted as a safe principle : Whenever the action of the verb does really pass over to the object, let the dative case be employed. Let not the student frame his practice merely on analogy. જણવું to bring forth, governs only an accusative.

It is important here to guard against an error that substantives signifying inanimate objects cannot consistently with the genius of the language take the dative. They do invariably take the dative when finality is to be expressed, as Ex. મે નદીમાં પથરને ડુબાડો I sunk *to* a stone in the river. મે ઝાહાડને ઉખેડું I rooted up *to* the tree. That they are less frequently found in this case, arises not from the fact that they denote inanimate objects, but that inanimate objects are less frequently the final objects of transitive action. They are not generally affected by the action of the verb. When they are so, the use of the dative is imperative

case formed by the post-fix of the preposition એ by, &c.* This may be called the Ablative or case denoting medium or instrumentality. Hence for practical purposes, though not with philosophical accu racy, the Gujaráti substantive may be said to have six cases.

GENDER.

Substantives have three genders, Masculine, Feminine, and Neuter. The two former in their *primary* use correspond to the two sexes of objectives in nature, and the third expresses either the absence or indeterminateness of sex. In their *secondary* use, they express conventional ideas of sex founded on fancied analogies

---

Finally, it is worthy of notice, that the personal pronouns are never used in the accusative but in the dative case. The reason of this is obvious and strikingly illustrates the above explanation of this case. When the person is the object of the verb it must necessarily be considered as affected by the action of the verb. The individual cannot but be the point to which the action passes over. It may be intermediate relatively to something or some person else, but yet relatively to the verb, it must be the final point of its action. The accusative which expresses no material relation, is therefore incapable of representing this relation. Hence the dative alone is employed.

Observe. The verb governing the dative is called in this work the final objective verb.

* The preposition એ has been assumed as the characteristic of the ablative for two reasons. 1. It comprehends in signification all the other prepositions having a medial import, as by, in, and with. 2. It acquires prominence from the important relation which it bears to the transitive verbs, to which it mostly subserves the purpose of a nominative (see the use of the case elucidated.) The prepositions થી or થકી from, &c. may be also assumed to place the substantive in the ablative case. (See Preposition).

between material objects. Subsequently they indicate conventional usage, founded on the analogy of verbal terminations.

Hence the gender of words is deducible from, conjointly, the sex of the objects they signify, from conventional usage, and from verbal terminations. Conventional use is in its nature arbitrary, and sometimes contrary to that of other languages, even cognate ones. It cannot therefore be reduced to rigid rules. The following will guide the student into a sufficient acquaintance with gendral distinctions, for immediate practical purposes. Absolute experience alone can render him entirely conversant with them.

Promiscuous Rules for Gender, founded on signification and conventional usage.

1. Substantives significative of objects, whose sex is recognized as male or female, correspond in gender to such objects, irrespectively of termination.

Ex. મા mother. ભાઈ brother. બેહેન sister.

2. Substantives significative of individual objects *for the distinguishing of whose sex there is no appropriate form,* and having no gendral termination, are of common gender; that is, they are either masculine or feminine as may be intended to specify, but unless the specification of sex is intended, they are generally *masculine.*

Ex. વરૂ a wolf. ચાંચડ a flea.

Observe. Custom itself is not uniform. Pure Gújaráti words generally are of gendral terminations.

3. Substantives significative of genera of animals or species,

comprehending the two sexes, are neuter irrespectively of termination.

Ex. માણુશ man. ઢોર cattle. પંખી bird.

Observe. The same word may be of different genders, according as it is used for an individual or a species.

4. Substantives signifying the days of the week and the month of the year, are *masculine*. (See Promiscuous Tables).

5. Substantives signifying the lunar days are feminine. (See Prom. Tables). Except પડવો, the first day.

6. Substantives signifying the chief portions of the day, are of feminine gender ; as follows,

Ex. શવાર morning. પોહોર 8th part of a day. શાંજ evening.
ઘડી ghăḍí. રાત night.

7: Substantives signifying the four points of the Compass, are neuter; as follows,

ઊતર north. પશ્ચમ west.
દખ્શણ south. પુરવ east.

Observe. These are frequently used with દીશા, region, &c. which is feminine.

8. Substantives, which are the names of rivers are feminine.

Excep. When they have a masculine termination, in which case they are masculine. Ex. જાંબો Jambo, a river near Baroda.

9. The following substantives signifying the grander objects of the material world, are of gender as follows:

Masculine

શુરજ sun.	દરીઆ } sea	વા } wind.	પ્રવત } mountain,
ચંદ્ર moon.	શમુદર }	પવન }	ડુંગર }
ગ્રહ planet.			પાહાડ } hill.

Feminine.

પ્રથવી earth. જગત world. ધરતી earth. જમીન earth.

Neuter.

આકાશ sky.

10. Names of the members and organs of the body are of gender, as follows:

Mas.	*Fem.*	*Neuter.*
કાન ear	આંખ eye	મોહો mouth
હાથ hand	જાંગ thigh	તાળવું palate
પગ foot	નશ vein	પેટ belly
હોટ lip	પાપણ eyelid	ઘુંટણ knee
દાંત tooth	ખાંધ shoulder	નાક nose
નખ nail.	જીભ tongue.	કપાલ forehead.

Observe. The names which have gendral terminations are excluded from the above list.

11. Names of fruits are chiefly neuter.

Ex. નાલીએર cocoanut. લીંબુ lime.

12 Names of the species of grains are of gender, as follows:

Mas.	*Fem.*
મઠ	બાજરી
મગ	જુઆર
અરદ	દગિર
કોદરા	તુએર.
તલ	
ઘઊં.	

A few are neuter.

13. The names of countries, cities, towns, and villages are generally neuter. Ex. અમદાવાદ Ahmedabad.

Observe. It *sometimes* happens that the gendral termination decides the gender.

Rules for Masculine Gender founded on termination.

1. Substantives ending in the vowel ઓ are masculine irrespectively of signification.

Ex. હીરો a diamond. દરવાજો a door.

Observe. 1. This termination is the appropriate masculine form of the language. Not only does it belong to substantives but adjectives, pronouns, and several tenses of the verb, besides the preposition નો. It is the termination of substantives signifying inanimate objects, as well as of those signifying animals. As a general rule, whatever substantive of this termination has a feminine form in ઈ, is conceived of as possessing *male* qualities.

Ex. ખાટલો a cot, has a feminine form ખાટલી. It is therefore of larger size and more robust make than it. (See Remarks on the feminine termination ઈ).

Observe. 2. Some Hindústáni substantives in આ are changed into ઓ in Gujaráti, and become masculine, although the original word was feminine. Ex. દરીઓ sea. દુનીઓ world. دریا دنیا

Exception.—A few monosyllables.

2. Substantives ending in ત, preceded by the anusvara derived from the Sanscrit, are mostly masculine.

Ex. દાંત tooth.

3. Substantives consisting of active verbal roots as also of causatives, are mostly masculine.

Ex. મારમાર beating. ધમકાવ threatening.

Rules for Feminine Gender, founded on termination conjointly with signification.

1. Substantives from the Sanscrit ending in આ (signifying abstractness).

Ex. આશા hope. અવસ્થા circumstance.

2. Substantives from the Sanscrit ending in તા (signifying abstract quality).

Ex. શુધતા purity.

3. Gujaráti substantives ending in આઈ, આશ, ક, આત, (signifying abstract quality).

Ex. મીઠાઈ sweetness. કડવાશ bitterness. ઠંડક cold. કઠણાત hardness.

4. Substantives ending in ણી, a suffix to a verbal root.

Ex. શીવણી, a sewing.

5. Substantives from the Hindústáni, ending in શ, દ, ત, ગી (signifying abstractness).

Ex. તપાશ enquiry. તાકીદ importunity. તબીયત constitution. તાજગી freshness. There are some exceptions.

6. Substantives from the Hindústáni in જ, sounded as z, being the representative of ز

Ex. ચીજ thing. ઈલાજ remedy. નીમાજ religious service.

7. Substantives from Hindústáni, ending in આ, (signifying abstractness).

Ex. સજા punishment, ઈજા injury.

8. Gujaráti Substantives ending in ઈ (signifying objects, as also abstractness).

Ex. પેટી box. ડાળી branch. પટેલી Patelship.

Exception. 1. The following are neuter, as also a few other monosyllables:

પાણી	water
બી	seed
ઘી	ghí
સોપારી	betel
મરી	pepper

Exception. 2. Such as are deducible from rules of signification.

Observe. This termination, the appropriate feminine form of this language, is of equal latitude in the range of its application with the masculine form ઓ. It is derivable from all substantives in ઓ, whether signifying animate or inanimate objects. If the latter, it denotes a diminutive species or quality, analogous to those of the female sex; such as delicate frame, texture, &c.

Ex. from શીશો a bottle, derive શીશી a vial.

9. Substantives ending in ઈણ, આણી, ણી (being appropriate feminine forms of masculine substantives, see Gender Table).

10. Substantives formed by the duplication of a neuter verbal root, are very frequently feminine.

Ex. કચકચ grumble. બડબડ mutter.

11. Substantives ending in આખ, or આંખ, are mostly feminine.

Ex. પાંખ wing. રાખ ashes.

Rules for Neuter Gender founded on termination conjointly with signification, or on termination alone.

1. Substantives ending in ઉં are neuter irrespectively of signification.

Ex. કુતરૂં dog. ગાડું cart.

Observe. This termination is the neuter characteristic of the language, and it is formable from all substantives ending in ઓ. When the termination of substantives denoting inanimate objects, it expresses the idea of clumsiness, and roughness of make.

2. Substantives ending in પણુ, or પણું, signifying abstractness of condition, &c.

Ex. ઘડપણુ old age. ડાહાપણું wisdom.

3. Substantives ending in આણુ formed from adjectives signifying abstractness.

Ex. ઉંડાણુ depth.

4. Substantives ending in ણુ, મણુ, being a suffix to a verbal root.

Ex. ચલણુ conduct. શીખામણુ instruction.

5. Substantives ending in આણું being suffix to a verbal root.

Ex. ઊઘરાણું collection.

Declension.

1. All substantives are reducible under two classes, viz. those which have *no* oblique form at all in their cases, whether with

or without prepositions, and those which *have* such oblique form.

2. The former class may for the sake of distinction and reference be called the First Declension.

3. The latter class may, from the same reasons, be called the Second Declension.

4. The first declension comprises all monosyllables* of whatever termination, and all other substantives of whatever termination, save the vowel અો and the vowel ઉ when headed by the anusvara. This declension forms its plural by the suffix of the vowel અો. If the final letter be a consonant this vowel is suffixed in its coalescent form. If the final letter be a vowel it is suffixed in its isolate form.

The second declension comprises all substantives not monosyllables, having final અો and ઉં. The substantive of this declension changes its final અો and ઉં into આ, which may be called its oblique form. To the substantive thus modified all suffixes for case or number are attached.

If the final letter be અો the plural is formed by suffixing અો to the oblique form આ. If the final letter be ઉં the plural is formed by merely suffixing the point to the oblique form,—that is by converting આ into આં.

---

* Under monosyllables are classed words whose consonant is followed by an isolate as a well as coalescent vowel; thus ઘઉં wheat, is a monosyllable as well as ઘી ghí. There may be even two vowels following the consonant provided that they are diphthongal, not demanding a new configuration of the organs.

SUBSTANTIVE.

First Declension.

FINAL CONSONANT.

Singular.			*Plural.*		
Without Prepositions.			*Without Prepositions.*		
Nom.	નામ	a name.	*Nom.*	નામો	names.
Ac.	નામ	a name.	*Ac.*	નામો	names.
Voc.	નામ	* O name!	*Voc.*	નામો	O names!
With Prepositions.			*With Prepositions.*		
Gen.	નામનો	† of a name.	*Gen.*	નામોનો	of names.
Dat.	નામને	to a name.	*Dat.*	નામોને	to names.
Ab.	નામે	‡ by a name.	*Ab.*	નામોએ	by names.

FINAL VOWEL.

Singular.			*Plural.*		
Without Prepositions.			*Without Prepositions.*		
Nom.	મા	a mother.	*Nom.*	માઓ	mothers.
Ac.	મા	a mother.	*Ac.*	માઓ	mothers.
Voc.	મા	O mother!	*Voc.*	માઓ	O mothers!

---

* The vocative may be preceded by the interjections અરે, ઓ, &c. answering to the English O, oh!

† For declination of the preposition નો, see Preposition.

‡ Observe. If the final letter of the substantive be a consonant, the ablative form એ is suffixed in its coalescent form. 2. The sign of the ablative એ is thrown back instead of being a suffix in the ablative of ઘર, which is not generally ઘરે but ઘેર.

નો masc., ની fem., નુ neu.
ના નાં

With Prepositions.			*With Prepositions.*		
Gen.	માનો	of a mother.	*Gen.*	માઓનો	of mothers.
Dat.	માને	to a mother.	*Dat.*	માઓને	to mothers.
Ab.	માએ	* by a mother.	*Ab.*	માઓએ	by mothers.

Second Declension.

Final આ.

Singular.			*Plural.*		
Without Prepositions.			*Without Prepositions.*		
Nom.	છોકરો	a boy.	*Nom.*	છોકરાઓ ‡	boys.
Ac.	છોકરો	a boy.	*Ac.*	છોકરાઓ	boys.
Voc.	છોકરા	O boy!	*Voc.*	છોકરાઓ	O boys!
With Prepositions.			*With Prepositions.*		
Gen.	છોકરાનો	of a boy.	*Gen.*	છોકરાઓનો	of boys.
Dat.	છોકરાને	to a boy.	*Dat.*	છોકરાઓને	to boys.
Ac.	છોકરાએ	† by a boy.	*Ab.*	છોકરાઓએ	by boys.

* Observe. 1. If the final letter be a vowel, the ablative suffix એ is put in its isolate form. 2. If the final letter be the vowel એ, the ablative form cannot be indicated in the usual way unless it be a monosyllable, e. g. ભાંએ ground, is both in the nominative and ablative forms.

Observe. All substantives of the same declension are declined as the above of whatever termination, as કવી a poet, બેહેન sister, આંખ eye, રાજા king, ચાપુ penknife, &c.

† This is the full and correct form of the ablative, but for the sake of euphony the penultimate vowel આ is dropped in some substantives. The ablative of દાહાડો is દાહાડાએ, but દાહાડે is substituted, &c.

‡ This is the full and correct form of the nominative plural, but the ઓ is sometimes dropped, when the substantive is qualified by any word indicating its plurality.—Thus for દીકરાઓ, કુતરાઓ, proper plurals દીકરા, કુતરા, with a plural adjective are commonly heard.

This is an unprecise mode of speech and should not be imitated.

FINAL ઉં.

Singular.			*Plural.*		
Without Prepositions.			*Without Prepositions.*		
Nom.	ઈંડું	an egg.	*Nom.*	ઈંડાં	eggs.*
Ac.	ઈંડું	an egg.	*Ac.*	ઈંડાં	eggs.
Voc.	ઈંડા	O egg!	*Voc.*	ઈંડાં	O eggs!
With Prepositions.			*With Prepositions.*		
Gen.	ઈંડાનો	of an egg.	*Gen.*	ઈંડાંનો	of eggs.
Dat.	ઈંડાને	to an egg.	*Dat.*	ઈંડાંને	to eggs.
Ab.	ઈંડાએ	by an egg.	*Ab.*	ઈંડાંએ	by eggs.

Substantives with Prepositions suffixed.

થી / થકી } from, by, with	are thus post-fixed to the substantives નામ and છોકરો	નામથી-નામથકી from, &c. a name. છોકરાથી-છોકરાથકી from, &c. a boy.
વાસતે / સારૂ / માટે } for		*With or without a Dative.* નામવાશતે-નામનેવાશતે for a name. છોકરાવાશતે-છોકરાનેવાશતે for a boy.
પાશે } to, or near		*With or without Genitive.* નામપાશે-નામનીપાશે near a name. છોકરાપાશે-છોકરાનીપાશે near a boy.
માં in		નામમાં in a name. છોકરામાં in a boy.

* The form ઈંડાંઓ is sometimes used but incorrectly. Its use arises from the oversight of the mindu.

This form is employed in token of respect, for the plural of substantives in ઈ e. g. for બાએડીઓ, which is the plural of બાએડી is substituted બાએડાં.

If the penultimate be an isolate vowel, the plural form આં is suffixed in its isolate form.

Ex. ખીઉં would make ખીઆં in the plural.

Prepositions are suffixed in the same way to the substantives in the plural number.

Lesson illustrative of Case and Number.

Observe. That the preposition નો follows the word signifying the *subject* of possession, and not as in English, the *object* of possession.

રાજા ની વાડીઓ નાં જાહાડો માં
king of gardens of trees in

પલંગ ના પાયાઓ નું લાકડું
bedstead of feet of wood

માણુશ ના મન નો વીચાર
man of mind of thought

અંગ ની ચાંમડી નાં રૂઆં
body of skin of hair

વડ ની ડાળીઓ નાં પાંતરાં ને
banyan of branches of leaves to

વાડી ના ચાકરો ને શારૂ
garden of servants to for

શરકાર ના શીપાઈઓ ની
Government of soldiers of

બંદુકો થી તથા તીરો થી
guns with and arrows with

ઘોડા ની રીકાબો નું લોહોડું
horse of stirrups of iron

શેહેર ની દુકાનો માં
city of shops in

પુશતક નાં પાનાં નો રંગ
book of leaves of colour

કોટડી ના દરવાજાઓ
room of doors

ADJECTIVE.

1. The adjective is used for two purposes in this language, viz. those of qualifying a substantive and adjective.* It therefore possesses partly the nature of an adverb.

2. Adjectives are reducible under two classes on the same principle of classification as that of the substantive, viz. the capacity or incapacity of taking an oblique form. (See Substantive).

* The same word often qualifies both the substantive and adjective, e. g. ઘણું પાંણી much water. 2. ઘણું ગરમ પાંણી very hot water.

3. Adjectives, of the first declension, comprise all with whatever termination save ઓ. They are indeclinable for gender, number and case.*

4. Adjectives, of the second declension, comprise all ending in ઓ. They are declinable for gender, number and case.

5. They admit of only one inflection for case, viz. the change of ઓ into આ, not being susceptible as substantives of prepositional cases.

6. The inflections for gender correspond to the three great gendral distinctions of substantives, viz. ઓ mas. ઈ fem. and ઉં neuter; sustaining these gendral forms, they are declinable like the substantives.

7. If the adjective be used as a substantive or predicatively, the inflections for number are frequently the same as those of substantives of the same respective terminations. If the adjective be used strictly adjectively, the mere oblique form of the adjective in ઓ and the original form of the adjective in ઈ are used, while the neuter plural is the same as that of the substantive plural of the same termination.

The following declension, of an adjective of the second declension with substantives of corresponding gender, will amply illustrate the above rules.

---

* It is evident that if a preposition be post-fixed to the adjective, or if the adjective be used in the plural form without a substantive, it ceases to be in sense an adjective, and becomes a substantive. The above rule therefore applies only to adjectives as adjectives. Let it be understood once for all, that adjectives of either declension used substantively, are declinable as substantives.

Adjective in the Masculine form with a Masculine Substantive.

સારો ઘોડો A GOOD HORSE.*

Singular.	*Plural.*
Without Prepositions.	*Without Prepositions.*
Nom. સારો ઘોડો.	*Nom.* સારા ઘોડાઓ.
Ac. સારો ઘોડો.	*Ac.* સારા ઘોડાઓ.
Voc. સારા ઘોડા.	*Voc.* સારા ઘોડાઓ.
With Prepositions.	*With prepositions.*
Gen. સારા ઘોડાનો.	*Gen.* સારા ઘોડાઓનો.
Dat. સારા ઘોડાને.	*Dat.* સારા ઘોડાઓને.
Ab. સારા ઘોડાએ. †	*Ab.* સારા ઘોડાઓએ.

Adjective in the Feminine form with a Feminine Substantive.

સારી છોકરી A GOOD GIRL.

Singular.	*Plural.*
Without Prepositions.	*Without Prepositions.*
Nom. સારી છોકરી.	*Nom.* સારી છોકરીઓ. ‡
Ac. સારી છોકરી.	*Ac.* સારી છોકરીઓ.
Voc. સારી છોકરી.	*Voc.* સારી છોકરીઓ.

Although substantives with gendral forms are given as examples, the declension of the adjective is in no wise dependent on the declension of the substantive. E. G. સારી કલમ, a good pen.

† If the ultimate of the substantive be a consonant with the suffix એ, the adjective likewise takes the ablative form. E. G. સારેદીશે on a good day મોહોટે દાહાડે, &c. on a great day.

‡ The natives frequently use the form સારીઓ predicatively, as the chiming of the sound with the substantive pleases them. Thus, આ છોકરીઓ સારીઓ છે These girls are good.

If the substantive have the neuter plural of respect, the adjective must correspond with it.—Thus, સારાં બાએડાં good women.

With Prepositions.	*With Prepositions.*
Gen. સારી છોકરીનો.	*Gen.* સારી છોકરીઓનો.
Dat. સારી છોકરીને.	*Dat.* સારી છોકરીઓને.
Ab. સારી છોકરીએ.	*Ab.* સારી છોકરીઓએ.

Adjective in the Neuter form with a Neuter Substantive.

સારૂં ગાડું A GOOD CART.

Singular.	*Plural.*
Without Prepositions.	*Without Prepositions.*
Nom. સારૂં ગાડું.	*Nom.* સારાં ગાડાં.
Ac. સારૂં ગાડું.	*Ab.* સારાં ગાડાં.
Voc. સારા ગાડા.	*Voc.* સારાં ગાડાં.
With Prepositions.	*With Prepositions.*
Gen. સારા ગાડાનો.	*Gen.* સારાં ગાડાંનો.
Dat. સારા ગાડાને.	*Dat.* સારાં ગાડાંને.
Ab. સારા ગાડાએ.	*Ab.* સારાં ગાડાંએ.

DEGREE.

Adjectives have no peculiar form to express either the comparative or superlative degrees. This defect is supplied in the following ways.

1. Adjectives significative of degree (either below or above the positive) are conjoined with the adjective expressing the quality.

Ex. વતું સારૂં better; ઘણું ખોટું very bad; થોડું ગરમ little hot.

2. In order to express comparison with another object, the preposition થી from, or કરતાં than, is fixed to the word expressing the object, and the adjective follows.

Ex. 1. હું તેથી સારોછુજ I am better than he.

2. પશુ કરતાં હું બુધીવાનછુજ I am wiser than a beast.

3. If the quality is intended to be expressd as existing in at much greater degree, a word signifying more, very, &c. is added to the adjective.

Ex. હું તમારા કરતાં વતેા ડાયેા છુજ I am much wiser than you.

4. The quality of the adjective possessed in a very faint degree is expressed by suffixing the numeral એક, or its curtailed form ક, or by prefixing the pronoun કંઈ.

કાલુંએક blackish; કંઈભણેલેા somewhat learned.

Reading Lesson.

સારાં છેાકરાં ની ચેાપડીએા	રુપા ના લાંબા કાંટાએા
good children of books	silver of long forks
કાલા માંણુશ નું રુપ	ઊંડા કુવા નું પાંણી
black man of countenance	deep well of water
ખાટી કેરીએા મીઠાં અંજીરેા	ઊંચા જાડ ના મુલ માં
sour mangoes sweet figs	high tree of root in
ઊંચા પાહાડ ની ટેાચ	ગાંમેા ની સારી વશતીએા માં
high hill of top	villages of good habitations in

Note. There is no word significative of degree corresponding to the English "too." Hence the learner finds considerable difficulty in expressing this idea so frequently reverting to the mind. The lack of such a term is supplied in two ways:

1. By the use of the superlative which from the circumstances of use may by implication suggest the idea of "too," especially if a stress be laid upon the word. Ex. તમે ઘણું ઊતાવલું બેાલેા છેા you speak very fast (i. e. by implication *too* fast).

2. By a periphrasis declaring the bounds transgressed, as of propriety, necessity, &c. Ex. જેાઈએ તે કરતાં વતેા વરસાદ થએા There has been too much rain (more than is needed).

મોહોટા શેહેર ના લોકો
large city of people

ગરમ લુગડાં ની કીમત
warm clothes of price

મોંઘી બાજરી ના દાણાઓ
dear millet of grains

સસતું રેસમ નું લુગડું
cheap silk of cloth

રાતા ઘોડા ની આંખો
red horse of eyes

ધોલી ગાએ નું દુધ
white cow of milk

નરમ રોટલી નો આટો
soft bread of flour

મોહોટી પેટી ના ખીલાઓ*
large box of nails

લીલાં જાડો નાં લીલાં પાતરાં
green trees of green leaves

ધોલા હાથી ના મોહોટા કાનો
white elephant of large ears

સારા છોકરા નાં મોંઘાં રમકડાં
good child of dear toys

આકાશ ના ચમકતા તારાઓ
sky of glittering stars.

જુદા દેશો ના શરસતાઓ
different countries of customs

તથા રીતો
and manners

Pronouns.

The Pronouns of this language are reducible under four classes.

1. Personal Pronouns or those which represent persons or things. These necessarily comprehend their genitive cases, in which form they become possessive pronouns.

2. Definitive Pronouns or those which define objects, their quality, quantity, &c.

3. Interrogative Pronouns or those which are a medium of interrogation as to objects, quality, quantity, &c.

Note. Adjectival pronouns, when used as substantives, are like them susceptible of prepositional cases and number. When used as adjectives in qualifying substantives, they are altogether declinable like adjectives, according to their termination.

4. Relative Pronouns or those which have relation either anticipatively or respectively to a substantive, either expressed or understood. These involve their correlates.

1. Personal Pronouns.

These are undeclinable for gender, being in their origina form, masculine, feminine, and neuter. They are declined for case and number as follows:

1st Person. હું.

Singular.	*Plural.*
m. f. n.	*m. f. n.*
Nom. હું I.	*Nom.* હમે or હમો we‡.
*Ac.**	*Ac.*
Gen. માહારો, &c.† of me or my.	*Gen.* હમારો, &c. of us, or our.
Dat. મને to me.	*Dat.* હમને, or હમોને to us.
Ab. મે by me.	*Ab.* હમે, or હમોએ by us.

Additional form taken from the Possessive Pronouns.§

Singular.	*Plural.*
Dat. / *Ab.* } માહારે to or by me.	*Dat.* / *Ab.* } હમારે to or by us.

* For the reason of Accusative, being wanting, See Remarks on Acc.

† This is the possessive pronoun and is declined as an adjective.

‡ This plural is often used for dignity, instead of the singular.

§ This is used both as a dative and ablative. It is doubtful whether it cannot be resolved wholly into the ablative. The form મને signifies *me,* in my individuality. The form માહારે signifies me, in my possession, i. e. in what belongs to me, duty, obligation, &c. Its chief use as an ablative is with the infinitive mood. Ex. માહારે જવું જોઇએ by me it is necessary to go. This form is also the ablative of the possessive, signifying by my, e. g. માહારે ઘેર at my house. It must not be confounded with its use as a personal pronoun.

2nd. Form. (Plural) *.

આપ self. (Obsolete) †.

	m. f. n.	
Nom.	આપણે	we.
Gen.	આપણનો &c.	of us ‡.
Dat.	આપણને	to us.
Ab.	આપણે	by us.

2nd Person. તું

Singular. m. f. n.			*Plural.* m. f. n.		
Nom.	તું	thou §.	*Nom.*	તમે or તમો	you ¶.
Gen.	તાહારો, &c.	of thee, thy ‖.	*Gen.*	તમારો, &c.	of you.
Dat.	તને	to thee.	*Dat.*	તમને or તમોને	to you.
Ab.	તેં	by, &c. thee.	*Ab.*	તમે or તમોએ	by you.

---

* The first form હમે is used throughout all its cases when the person addressing does not comprehend the person addressed with himself. The second form is used throughout all its cases when the person addressing comprehends with himself the person addressed. Two beautiful illustrations of these two forms are found in the Gospel of John, 7. chap. 5. ver. "Doth our Law," &c.. Here the second form આપણો is used, because Nicodemus comprehended the Sanhedrim whom he addressed with himself. The other form is illustrated in John 19: 7. "By our Law," &c. Here the first form હમારો must be used, because the Jews did not comprehend Pilate with themselves.

† આપ is sometimes used for respect instead of the second personal plural, as આપ કાંહાં જાઓછો ? Where are you going ?

‡ Declinable as an adjective in the contracted form આપણો ણી ણું our.

§ This singular form is addressed, 1. to inferiors; 2. occasionally as a mark of affection; 3. in familiarity; 4. in addresses to God.

‖ See note on મને.

¶ The possessive pronoun, declinable.

ADDITIONAL FORM.*

Singalar.	*Plural.*
Dat. } *Ab.* } તાહારે to or by thee.	*Dat.* } *Ab.* } તમારે to or by you.

3RD PERSON.

એ and તે He, She, or It.

Singular. *m. f. n.*	*Plural.* *m. f. n.*
Nom. તે he, &c.	*Nom.* તેઓ they.
Ac. તે it.	*Ac.* તેઓ them (neuter).
Gen. તેનો, of him, &c.†	*Gen.* તેઓને of them.
Dat. તેને, to him, &c.	*Dat.* તેઓને to them.
Ab. તેણે, by him, &c.	*Ab.* તેઓએ by them.

એ is declined in the same way. These as well as આ are used as definitive Pronouns.

તે is likewise the correlate of જે (see જે).

REFLECTIVE PRONOUN.

પોતે Self or Selves.

1ST. 2ND. AND 3RD. PERSON.

Singular and Plural.

m. f. n.

Nom. પોતે self or selves.

Voc. પોતે o self, &c.

* This plural form is in general use for respect, instead of the singular.

† The possessive pronoun declinable.

Gen. પોતાનો of self, &c. *
Dat. પોતાને to self, &c.
Ab. પોતે by self, &c.

Reflective Pronoun.

Singular and *Plural* પોત પોતે each respectively,

It is declined like પોતે.

Ex. 1. તેઓ પોત પોતાને ઘેર ગયા. They went each to his own house.

---

* The possessive pronoun, own, declinable.

NOTE. This pronoun may be used with either of the personal pronouns both singular and plural, as હું પોતે I myself, તું પોતે thou thyself, તે પોતે he himself, i. e. exclusively of other persons, and so on through all the cases. But in the genitive case it has a somewhat modified meaning. It does not then denote possession by one's self as exclusively of others in a sense corresponding to the English "own," but it denotes the simple idea of belonging to self without any extraneous idea of peculiar appropriation. By its use it merely refers the thing possessed to the possessor, and precludes the reference of it to another party; Ex. તે પોતાનો હાથ ઉચકેછે he lifts his hand, (literally the hand of self). Here the idea expressed is not, that he lifts *his own* and not another person's hand, but merely that *he*, the subject of the verb, lifts the hand of *him* the same subject. Reference to any one foreign to the subject is prevented. In English, were the expression used, "he lifts his hand", it would be doubtful whether the person lifted his own hand or the hand of some one else.

Such ambiguity is frequent in English, but it is entirely removed in Gujaráti by the respective uses of these pronouns. Were it written તેનો હાથ, it would certainly mean that he lifted the hand of *another* person.

This method of distinguishing persons must be acknowledged a great beauty in the language, and recognition of it is requisite to a good translation.

Pronouns with Preposition suffixed.

With હું.

થી } from, &c. થકી }	હુંથી મજથી } from, &c. me માહારાથી માહારેથી }
વાશતે for.	માહારે વાશતે for me.
પાસે near, to.	માહારી પાશે near, to me.
માં in.	માહારા માં in me.

With તું	*With* તે
તુંથી-તજથી } from, &c. thee. તાહારાથી-તાહારેથી }	તેથી-તેનાથી from him, &c.
તાહારે વાસતે for thee.	તે વાશતે-તેને વાશતે for him, &c,
તાહારી પાશે near to thee.	તેપાશે-તેનીપાશે near to him.
તાહારામાં in thee.	તેમાં-તેનામાં in him, &c.

With આપણુ.	*With* પોતે.
આપણુથી-આપણુાથી from us.	પોતાથી-પોતાનાથી from self, &c.
આપણેવાસતે for us.	પોતેવાશતે-પોતાનેવાશતે for self, &c.
આપણીપાસે near to us.	પોતાનીપાંશે near to self, &c.
આપણુામાં in us.	પોતામાં-પોતાનામાં in self, &c.

2. Definitive Pronouns.

1st. *of Object.*

આ એ this }
તે that } are declined as the personal pronouns.

પેલા That yonder, is declined as an adjective.

આ expresses proximity, એ expresses proximity less proximate, તે express remoteness, પેલા further remoteness. Although તે

and પેલા are classed among definitive pronouns, they sometimes correspond in power to the English Definite Article.

They do this when they define in the fact of previous cognizance; Ex. તે or પેલા ભીખારી કાલે આવેા હતો may be rendered, "*The* beggar came yesterday" i. e the beggar of whom there was cognizance in some way or other. These pronouns cannot be used as the English *the* when it is used to specify a class; as, *the* Hindus, *the* Persians, &c. nor to express monadity, as *the* Sun, *the* Stars, &., but are used to specify individuals.

આ એ તે have prolonged feminine forms, which are used with only a few words, as ગમ બાજુ signifying side, direction.

These forms are આણી એણી તેણી. These forms seem used for intensity of demonstration, and answer to the English vulgar form of *this here, that there.*

The following are indeclinable for Gender and Number, but declinable for Case, as a Substantive:

કોઈ any, some (person or thing), હર કોઈ any whatever, (person or thing).

કંઈ * any, some (thing); હરકંઈ any, whatever (thing).

એક એક each (person or thing), હરએક હરેક every one (person or thing).

કોઈએક † any, some *one* (person or thing); કંઈએક any, some *one* (thing).

---

* કંઈ is not the neuter of કોઈ, as it may be used with a feminine, કંઈ વસ્તુ some thing.

† કોઈએક means some *one* or another. The particular one needs not or cannot be specified. It may be translated occasionally by "a certain," which the frequent power of એક (see Remarks on Article).

2. *Of quality, quantity, kind.*

(Declinable for gender, number and case).

m.	*f.*	*n.*		*m.*	*f.*	*n.*	
આવો	વી	વું	so (in quality.	એવો	વી	વું	so, &c
આટલો	લી	લું	so (in quantity).	એટલો	લી	લું	so, &c.
આવડો	ડી	ડું	so (in kind).	એવડો	ડી	ડું	so, &c.

3. Interrogative Pronouns.

1st. *Of things and persons.*

(Declinable for case).

	m.	*f.*	*n.*			*m.*	*f.*	*n.*	
Sing.	શો	શી	શું	what?	*Sing.*	કહો	કહી	કહું	which?
Plur.	શા	શી	શાં	what?	*Plur.*	કહા	કહી	કહાં	which?

કહો has a feminine form કેણી corresponding in use to એણી, as કેણીગમ which side?

Singular.			*Plural.*		
	m. f. n.			*m. f. n.*	
Nom.	કોણ	who?	*Nom.*	કોણો	whom?
Gen.	કોણનો	of whom?	*Gen.*	કોણોનો	of whom?
Dat.	કોણને	to whom?	*Dat.*	કોણોને	to whom?
Ab.	કોણે	by whom?	*Ab.*	કોણોએ	by whom?

2. *Of quality, quantity, and kind.*

(Declinable for gender, number, case).

m.	*f.*	*n.*	
કેહેવો	વી	વું	of what quality?
કેટલો	લી	લું	how much?
કેવડો	ડી	ડું	of what kind?

4. Relative Pronouns.

1. *Person and Thing.*

જે who, which, what.*

m. f. n.

Singular.			*Plural.*		
Nom.	જે	who, &c.	*Nom.*	જેઓ	who, &c.†
Ac.	જે	who, &c.	*Ac.*	જેઓ	who, &c.
Gen.	જેનો	of whom, &c.	*Gen.*	જેઓનો	of whom, &c.
Dat.	જેને	to whom, &c.	*Dat*	જેઓને	to whom, &c.
Ac.	જેણે	by whom, &c.	*Ab.*	જેઓએ	by whom, &c.

* The plural form is not retained before a substantive.

† This pronoun in most examples differs in position from the English relative *who*, but agrees with it in power.—The following sentences illustrate both its power and its position. 1. "At *what* time ye hear." 2. "*Who* is wise will understand." This pronoun is both anticipative and reflective, differing in its power according to its respeotive uses.—1. In the following example this pronoun is an anticipative relative. જે માણસને તમે મોકલ્યો the man whom you sent. This is a specimen of the general use of જે. What is its syntactical power? It is simply a copula or connecting link between માણસ and મોકલ્યો, (in a way analogous to the Greek article or demonstrative), connecting the two elements into one complex subject, which but for it would have been a complete

The correlate is તે, he, she, it,

Relative.	*Correlate.*

જે જે whoever, &c. specifically તે તે he, &c.

જે કોઈ whoever, &c. (person and thing.) જે કંઈ whatever (thing.)	Individually.

There is also a feminine form જેણી corresponding to એણી in use; as જેણી ગમ whichever side. The correlate is તેણી.

2. *Of quality, quantity, kind.*

(Declinable for gender, number and case.)

Relatives.				*Correlates.*			
m.	*f.*	*n.*		*m.*	*f.*	*n.*	
જેવો	વી	વું	as (in quality).	તેવો	વી	વું	so, &c.
જેટલો	લી	લું	as (in quantity).	તેટલો	લી	લું	so, &c.
જેવડો	ડી	ડું	as (in kind).	તેવડો	ડી	ડું	so, &c.

---

sentence, and qualifying it to be the subject of the following predicate which is headed by the correlate. If this view of its power be correct, then it follows that this pronoun does not distribute. It does not sygnify "whoever." This is the province of જે જે which necessarily distributes. It is not denied that જે may be often rendered by whoever.—But they are not equivalent. *It does not by its own intrinsic power refer the object to which it relates (whether expressed or understood) to a class.* The object may or may not be one of a class but the use of this pronoun does not elicit the fact. In the following Examples,

1. જે સમુદર સુકતો નથી તે &c. the sea which does not dry up, &c.
2. જે સુરજ નદીઓને સુકાવેછે &c. the sun which dries up the river, &c.

Verb.

Verbs need to be considered by the student of this language,

1. As to their structure.
2. As to the nature of the action they signify.
3. As to their conjugation or the inflections which they undergo for the representation of mood, tense, &c.

A comprehension of these three particulars is essential to an adequate perception of the genius of the language and to the purposes of its application in conversation and composition.

There is precluded all distribution, the ideas being monadic. The pronoun in these two examples has the same power as it has in the above cited, viz. it serves as a copula. This pronoun therefore may precede any word denoting monadity, as God, father, &c.

3. The following example illustrates the use of જે as a reflective,

ઈશ્વર જે તમારો ધણી છે તે કહેછે.

The syntactical power of the pronoun here is, that it places the words which it heads, with the word to which it relates in a state of apposition. ઈશ્વર is apposed with જે ધણીછે, so as to signify no more than the words ઈશ્વર and ધણી in apposition. Did the pronoun precede ઈશ્વર, it would make the sentence a complex subject. Being placed after it, ઈશ્વર is alone the simple subject, the other words being only in apposition. The reflective use generally expresses an after-thought. In rendering "I saw to-day the man whom you saw yesterday" the pronoun must precede "man." In rendering "I saw *a man* to-day whom you also saw yesterday," the pronoun must follow, "I saw a man to-day," as in English. Although the clause of the sentence may be rendered "him you also saw," yet the use of જે in such dependent sentences is very frequent.

1. Verbs of this language are either simple or compound.* Compound verbs consist of two or more verbs conjoined.

Ex. લખી રેહેવું to finish writing, is compounded of. લખવું to write, and રેહેવું to remain.

Verbs are compounded only of verbs. The language admits no other element of composition. Composition by prepositions so common to other languages, is unknown to Gujaráti.

2. Verbs are divisible according to their *signification*, as follows:

(1.) Intransitive† or verbs which signify action, *inhering in but not issuing from the agent*; or in other words, which express subjectiveness distinct from mediate agency. Such are verbs denoting existence either pure or modal; as, થવું to become, રેહેવું to remain; and reflective action, or action remaining only with the

---

* Many call certain nouns and verbs in their conjunct state compound verbs, as વીચાર કરવો to think (make thought), ગાળ દેવી to abuse (give abuse). This is erroneous. The noun is governed by the verb and is wholly distinct from the verb. We might on the same principle call every infinitive in English conjoined with a noun in the objective case, a compound verb; as, to give abuse, to do harm, &c. Again, many call a verb conjoined with an adjective a compound verb, as બંધ કરવું to shut. We might with equal propriety call such English expressions as, to make secure, to keep hot, &c. compound verbs. The Gujaráti employs nouns and adjectives with generic verbs to express specific actions for which it has no specific verbs, but in their conjunct state they are not to be called compound verbs. In such examples there is but *one* verb, and that is simple and governs its noun in the objective case.

† The terms, Transitive and Intransitive, do not express the exact nature of these verbs, which might be denominated subjective agents, and medial agents, but the definitions given will prevent erroneous conceptions.

agent, as ભણવું to learn. Such verbs may or may not express objectiveness, according as the signification of the verb may be, and therefore may or may not have an objective case.

This class of verbs recognizes the *agent alone as acting*, and not agency as proceeding from him. To denote this agent these verbs always have a nominative case in their aorist and aorist compound tenses, and are in this circumstance distinguished from verbs

(2.) Transitive, or verbs which signify *action issuing from the agent*, or in other words, which signify medial agency as distinguished from subjectiveness. Such verbs may be divided into two classes: 1st. Those whose action issues from the agent, but does not go forth to the object. These may be called simple objective verbs and always govern an accusative. 2nd. Those whose action not only issues from the agent but goes forth to its object. Such may be called final objective verbs and govern a dative case. Both classes reject in their past aorist tenses a nominative case, and in order to the representation of the mediality of agency, require the agent to be placed in the ablative case, and the object in either the accusative or dative according to the government of the verb * (see Ac. and Dat).

* The student will doubtless be perplexed with this principle of the language, and will be glad to receive any elucidation of the apparent anomaly of these two classes of verbs. Let him then first of all recognize the fact that the infinitive takes an ablative case of the substantive, in order to represent a medial agent. This principle reduced to terms simply expresses the formula " by a subject to do an action." The following example, માણુશોએ ઈશ્વર પર પરેમ રાખ-વો is resolvable into, By men to love God. Here there is no difficulty.

(3rd.) Passive verbs, or those significative of action, the object of which is identical with the subject of the verb, the subject sustaining the action of the verb e. g. હું પીડાએલ છું I am pained.

(4th.) Causative verbs, or verbs significative of action produced not directly by the subject of the verb, but medially through one

---

Now, if we remember that the aorist is nothing but a gerund denoting mere verbal action, with the superadded idea of past time, the application of the above principle will present no difficulty. Instead of the infinitive example which runs "By a subject to do an action," we must read "by a subject done an action," or according to the gerund formula, "by a subject was the doing of an action." The following example, માણુશોએ ઈશ્વર પર પરેમ રાખ્યો is resolvable into, "By men loved, or was loving to God." There seems therefore no difficulty in the case.

It has been assumed that the aorist is a gerund. That it is so, is evident from

1. It is not to be viewed as an impersonal verb, inasmuch as it agrees in gender and number with the object which it governs.

2. It is not passive, inasmuch as the object would on such a surmise be placed in the nominative, and not the objective. 3. It is not a participle, since were it, no reason would exist for its differing from the participle in એલો, in the fact of its being employed as a tense without the auxiliary. It is therefore a gerund. In intransitive verbs, the subject is considered as acting; the subject is therefore in the nominative, and by the fact of being preceded by a subject, the gerund assumes the nature of a tense. In transitive verbs, the gerund still remains, having no immediate subject, and agrees with its object. There is still one difficulty left, viz. why is not the object always placed in the dative case?

This difficulty may be met by asking, why is not the object by whatever verb and tense it may be governed, placed in the dative? When the accusative is governed, the sentence is resolvable into 1. Subject; 2. Action; 3. Object: but there is nothing to connect the action with the object. In the case of the aorist when governing an accusative, there is 1. Instrument; 2. Action; 3. Object: but nothing to indicate the transitiveness of the action. Both cases are parallel, and all that can be said is, it is a principle of the language. (See Remarks Dat. and Ac.)

or more media. e. g. ખવાડવું to cause to eat (one medium); ખવડાવવું to cause to cause to eat (two media).

3. Verbs whether simple or compound, neuter, active, passive or causative, are all conjugated in the same way. Hence there is, strictly speaking, but one conjugation.

The language for the purposes of Etymological changes recognizes but *one verb*, however verbs may differ in signification. This universal conjugation comprehends:

1. The Imperative; 2. The Infinitive with Gerunds and Participles; 3. The Indicative; 4. The Contingent (comprehending within itself the powers of the Subjunctive, the Potential and Conditional).

Before proceeding to the Regular Verb, it is advisable to study the auxiliary verb હો be. This differs in signification from the regular verb થવા in the following particular; હો signifies being or simple existence without reference to any thing extrinsic; થવા signifies being *inchoative*, or being taking its rise, involving inseparably the idea that before it was not.

The third person present of હોહો is the English copula. This verb is an auxiliary to થવા and to every other regular verb. It is defective and irregular.

Its participle and present tense are derived probably from a verb now obsolete.

It may here be remarked that there is no equivalent in the language to the English "have," but the place of this is supplied by this verb.

Ex. મ્હારી પાસે પઇશા છે literally, money *is* with me, i. e. I have money. It also supplies the place of that verb as an auxiliary, e. g. હું થયો છઉં I have been.

Remarks on the Auxiliary Verb, હો *Be.*

The infinitive is of unfrequent use, as થવું has been substituted. The adoption of it and of the gerund in its cases, is indispensable to correctness on some occasions.

The imperative is used only in a precative sense, and especially in the blessings so lavishly bestowed by Brámaṇs. There is a peculiarity about the imperative of all verbs when thus used, viz. that the verb does not agree with the nominative contained in the matter of precation, but is placed in the second person to agree with the person addressed.

Ex. ઈશ્વરની કીરપા તમને શદા હોજો may God's favour rest always on you. The present participle હોતો, is used chiefly if not wholly with a negative particle to form a second present tense. Ex. આ દેશમાં એવા લોક હોતા નથી no such people are (i. e. live, are found) in this country. The second participle છતાં signifies in, or during being, and is used :

1. As a genitive absolute.

Ex. માહારા છતાં તે હીયાંથી ગયો while I was, he went hence (in my being).

2. As a disjunctive conjunction, especially with the aorist of a verb.

Ex. શું તમે ભણ્યા છતાં નથી જાણતા? Do you not know, notwithstanding that you have studied?

The first present differs from the second, as follows:

The first expresses being present and actual, without reference to any thing extrinsic to itself, as of nature, habit, &c. and as unconnected with time in general.

Ex. 1. હું માંદો છુજી I am sick, i. e. now and actually, not naturally nor always.

The second is used as follows:

Ex. 2. આ દેશમાં હું મંદિ હોઉં છુઉં I am sick in this country, i. e. such is the habit of my constitution. Again માંણુશને બે પગ હોયેછે, man has two feet, i. e. such is his nature or constitution, in universal time.

The latter tense is therefore used to express universal quality, as inherent in sensible objects. The former is used to express moral maxims and principles (which from their nature are viewed as present and immutable). This tense alone can be used in propositions relative to God.

The imperfect is the equivalent of the English "was". It is also used in the latter clause of a conditional sentence, instead of હોત, and signifies were, would have been.

Ex. તે આવ્યો નહોત તો શરૂં હતું It would have been a good thing, if he had not come. The future is the same as the second present contingent.

Futurity and contingency can only be distinguished by the circumstances of use. When used in the first person, certainty is generally expressed—also when rendered definite by an adverb of time. Without some definitive words it is assumed to express contingency. The first present of the contingent, according to the power of that mood (see Con. M.), expresses:

1st. Mere hypothetical contingency, as is expressed in English by *be*.

Ex. જો તે તાંહાં નહોયે If he *be* not there.

2nd. Logical inference, as is expressed by "must" (in a dependent sentence).

Ex. જો તે માહારી મા હોયેતો હું તેનો દીકરો પણ હોઉં If she be my mother, I *must also be* her son.

3rd. What is compatible with the nature of things, as is expressed by "can," "could."

Ex. શું એ કામ ઈશ્વરને પશંદ હોએ? કદી નો હોએ *Can* this thing be pleasing to God? It *can* never be.

4th. Logical allowance, or something granted or supposed as expressed by *may*, let, granted that.

Ex. તે શેહેર વેગળું હોએ તોપણ માહારે તાંહાં જવું That city *may* be distant (granted) but I must go there.

5th. Allowance or permission, arising from indifference as is expressed by "*let*," ***but not injunction.***

Ex. જો એમ હોએ તો હોએ માહારે શું? If it be so, *let it be* so, what is that to me?

6th. In a dependent clause it is used to simply reiterate the meaning of the former clause, as is expressed by "*is.*"

Ex. જે કાળું હોએ તે કાળું હોએ ને જે ધોળું હોએ તે ધોળું હોએ What is black, *is* black, and what is white, *is* white.

7th. In an interrogative sentence, it frequently expresses incumbency, as expressed in English by *should.*

Ex. માહારો બાપ મુરખ હોય પણ હું કેમ હોઊં? My father may be a fool, but why *should* I be?

The second present contingent differs from the first in the fact that it expresses not hypothetical but circumstantial contingency. In a hypothetical clause it is rendered by "be," in the dependent clause by "may be," "can be," as also in an independent sentence.

Ex. 1. જો તે તાંહાં હોય તો તેની વહુ પણ તાંહાં હોય If he *be* there, his wife *may be* there also. 2. તે માહારી મા હોય પણ &c. She *may be* my mother, but &c.

It is also used in the same way as હોએ, in a reiterative sense, which see in 6th rule above.

The aorist according to its power (see Verb) is used to express:

1st. Mere hypothetical contingency, as by "were."

Ex. જો રાજા ધર્મશાલી હોત If the king *were* just.

2nd. Logical or circumstantial inference, as expressed by would, should, (in a dependent clause).

Ex. તો તેની પરજા શુખી હોત His subjects *would be* happy. This is a circumstancial inference, not a declaration of what would *ensue*, to express which થાત would be employed.

3rd. What is compatible with the nature of things as expressed by "could" (in any kind of sentence).

Ex. તે કાલે હીઆં હતો માટે તે તાંહાં કેમ હોત? He was here yesterday, how then *could he have been there?*

4th. Logical allowance, &c. as is expressed by "might."

Ex. તે માંદો હોત તે ખરો પણ &c. He *might be,* or *might have been* ill, but &c.

Observe, that the contingent tenses of this verb preclude intention of mind as expressed by "will" and as common to other verbs. This can be expressed only by the verb થા become.

Conjugation of the Auxiliary Verb હોહો *Be, (pure existence), irregular and defective.* *

હો Root of the Verb.

Imperative Mood.

Present Tense.

Singular.	*Plural.*
હો be thou.	હોઓ be ye.

* For the power of the tenses respectively study the preceding Remarks.

FUTURE.

હોજે be thou. | હોજો be ye.

Infinitive and Gerund.

હોવું be, being.*

Part. Noun. હોણાર be. er.

PARTICIPLES.

	m.	f.	n.			m.	f.	n.	
Sing.	હોતો	તી	તું	being.	*Sing.*	છુતો	તી	તું	being.
Plur.	હોતા	તી	તાં		*Plur.*	છુતા	તી	તાં	

Indecl. છુતાં being.

Indicative.

1ST PRESENT.

m. f. n.

Singular.	*Plural.*
હું છુઉં I am.	હમે છુઈએ we are.
તું છે thou art.	તમે છો you are.
તે છે he is.	તેઓ છે they are.

2ND PRESENT.

Singular.	*Plural.*
હું હોઉં છુઉં I am.	હમે હોઈએ છેઈએ we are.
તું હોએછે thou art.	તમે હોઓ છો you are.
તે હોએછે he is.	તેઓ હોએ છે they are.

---

* Let the gerund be declined as any other verb. Also let the infinitive be declined for gender. It is of seldom use.

IMPERFECT.

Singular.				*Plural.*			
m.	*f.*	*n.*		*m.*	*f.*	*n.*	
હું હતો	તી	તું	I was.	હમે હતા	તી	તાં	we were.
તું હતો	તી	તું	thou wast.	તમે હતા	તી	તાં	you were.
તે હતો	તી	તું	he was..	તેઓ હતા	તી	તાં	they were.

FUTURE.

Will and Shall.

m. f. n.

Singular.	*Plural.*
હું હોઈશ I will be.	હમે હોઈશે, શું we will be.
તું હોશે thou wilt be.	તમે હોશો you will be.
તે હોશે he will be.	તેઓ હોશે they will be.

Contingent Mood.

1ST PRESENT.

m. f. n.

Singular.	*Plural.*
હું હોઉં I may be, &c.	હમે હોઈએ we may, &c. be.
તું હોએ thou mayst be, &c.	તમે હોઓ you may, &c. be.
તે હોએ he may be, &c.	તેઓ હોએ they may, &c. be.

2ND PRESENT.

m. f. n.

Singular.	*Plural.*
હું હોઈશ I may be.	હમે હોઈશું we may be, (same as future).

Aorist.

m. f. n.

Singular.	*Plural.*
હું હોત I were, &c.	હમે હોત we were, &c.
તું હોત thou wert, &c.	તમે હોત you were, &c.
તે હોત he were, &c.	તેઓ હોત they were, &c.

Negative forms of Tenses.

1st.	Present	હું નથી	I am not.
2nd.	Present	હું હોતો-તી-તું નથી	I am not.
	Imperf.	હું નોહોતો-તી-તું	I was not.
	Imperf.	તું નહોતો-તી-તું	be thou not.

Remarks on Moods and Tenses of the Regular Verb, Transitive and Intransitive, with Illustrations.

Imperative.

Present. લખ 2nd. person, write thou—is the root of the verb to which every suffix is made.

Future. લખજે 2nd person, write thou—is especially used after the compound participle.

Ex. તાંહાં જઈને લખજે Lit. Having gone there, write.

This mood is used in the precatory sense, for curse or blessing.

Ex. તમારા છોકરાનો ઘણો આવરદા થાઓ May your child live long.

Infinitive, &c.

Present. લખવું to write, writing—is both infinitive and gerund. This is formed by adding વું to the root. As an infinitive it is susceptible of gender. As a gerund signifying the verbal action, it is placed in the neuter.

The following Examples illustrate both.

Ex. 1. તમારે શાચી વાત કેહેવી (infinitive) You *should speak* the truth.

Ex. 2. તમારૂં કેહેવું મને શારૂં લાગતું નથી (gerund) Your *saying* does not please me.

The infinitive is used 1. as the English infinitive, *when not expressing finality*. 2. With the auxiliary in the third person, to express action that either *is to* take place or *is desired to* take place.

Ex. 1. માહારે તાંહાં જવું છે I have to go there.

Ex. 2. તમારે ગુજરાતી ભાશા ભણવીછે? Do you wish to study Gujaráti?

3. To express obligation, duty, &c. in a sense equivalent to *must, should, ought.*

Ex. શરવે માબાપની મરીઆદા રાખવી All *should, &c.* obey their parents. See also the first example given under this mood.

This power is possessed also when the infinitive is used with an auxiliary.

Ex. તે કામ તમારે કરવું હતું You *ought to* have done that work.

4. As an imperative, to express a command or desire without harshness.

Ex. તમારે માહારે ઊંયાં આવવું Pray come to my house.

As a gerund it expresses invariably the verbal action, and is used in every respect as a substantive, being like it declinable with prepositions.

Ex. વીદીયા ભણવાથી ઘણો ગુણ થાએ છે There is much good from *studying* science.

The gerund in its genitive case, neuter gender, signifies ·

1. matter relating to verbal action.

Ex. મારારે તમને કેહેવાનું છે I have somewhat *to say* to you.

2· Incumbency, &c. especially in a negative sentence.

Ex. 1. તે ન બોલવાનું બોલ્યો He said what *ought* not *to be said*.

Ex. 2. આ કરવાનું કે નકરવાનું કામ છે Is this a work that *should*, or *should not* be done ?

3. It is used to qualify a substantive, where we should in English use an adjective, or express quality by "such as will."

Ex. આ મન બીગાડવાની વારતા છે This is a tale that would corrupt the mind (of corrupting).

4 It is used to express the several relations of the genitive case, which belongs to the substantive (see Genitive).

Ex. 1. તાંહાં જવાનો મારગ A road of going there (the road to that place).

Ex. 2. વીચાર કરવાની વાત A word of considering (a word worthy of consideration), &c.

The gerund in the dative expresses 1· verbal action final. It then becomes a supine. It has a curtailed form which is of equal signification with the full one.

Ex. હું જોવાને or હું જોવાં જાઊં છુઊં I am going to see.

1. When followed by a substantive it expresses the verbal action as subserving a purpose, where in English we use "for" and frequently a compound substantive.

Ex. 1. લખવાને પેટી A writing desk.

2. પીવાને પાણી Water for drinking.

Aorist Gerund. લખ્યું written—is formed by adding યું to the root. This is undoubtedly a gerund though generally conceived of as a participle. It is an element unknown to the English, and frequently demands a periphrastic rendering. It is capable of being the nominative of the verb, and is declinable with prepositions.

Ex. 1. માહારૂં કેહ્યું તેને લાગ્યું નહી *What I said* (my said) did not affect him.

2. માહારા કેહાથી તે કેમ શમજે How can he understand from *your said?* (what you said).

It remains for the reader to decide whether from the following example which exactly corresponds to the infinitive, this gerund be not likewise a past infinitive.

Ex. તમારે તે કાગલ લખ્યું જોઈએ You ought to have written that letter. Literally, By you that letter written ought.

Part. 1st. Present. લખતો—is formed by suffixing તો. It is declinable for gender and number. It is used occasionally in an adjectival sense, as ઊકલતું પાણી boiling water. It is used to express action taking place in present time, i. e. time present relatively to the verb with which it is conjoined.

Ex. મે તેને દોડતો જોયો I saw him running.

When repeated, it expresses reiterated action. This is the participial element of the compound tenses. Its signification is involved in the present tense, and hence of it there is no compound. This participle is used with a negative particle in the sense of the imperative, also with the particle નથી as a present tense negative, (see Conjugation). The plural neuter of this tense must not be confounded with

Part. 2nd. Present. લખતાં—writing (in). This is formed by adding તાં to the root. It expresses action in its process, and may be rendered by in, during, on. It is equivalent to a gerund with the preposition માં.

Ex. 1. મે તેને લખતાં જોયો I saw him writing, i, e. in the process.

Ex. 2. માહારા શાંભલતાં તેણે કહ્યું He said in my hearing.

It is used in the same way as a Genitive absolute ; as, તેના આ-વતાં હું તાંહાં જતો હતો As he was coming here, I was going there. When it has the participle જ suffixed, it expresses the exact point of time, as is expressed by "on."

Ex. તેનું શાંભલતાંજ હું ગયો On my hearing him I went.

When repeated, the process of action is represented as lengthened.

Ex. જગતમાં ફરતાં ફરતાં હું ઘણો ગનાન પાંમો છઉં Travelling about the world, I have obtained much knowledge.

This participle has frequently the force of a mere gerund, when signifying action considered as an art or science.

Ex, ગુજરાતી બોલતાં તમને આવડે છે Do you know how to talk Gujaráti ?

This last signification issues probably from the fact that the action which represents an art, does in its nature denote a process.

Part. Past. લખેલો written—is declinable. It is formed by suffixing એલો to the root. Probably this was એલ which is a suffix of the language. It signifies finished action in remote past time. This is an element of the compound tenses. This participle subserves in neuter verbs the use of the passives, but is not to be confounded with it. It also is used in active verbs where we should use the passive, but in such cases the medial agent in the ablative case is understood.

Ex. ઘોડો બાંધેલો હતો The horse was tied up. That is, Some one (understood) had tied up the horse.

It is often used as an adjective like the English participle.

Ex. ભણેલો પુરશ A learned man.

Compound Past. લખી or લખીને having written—is formed by suffixing ઈ or the more perfect form ઈને to the root. The former is used in the compounding of verbs. This participle signifies

1. Possession of finished action by some agent. It is used with another verb where we use two verbs in English connected by a conjunction.

Ex. પાતરૂં તોડીને પાણીમાં નાંખો Break off a leaf, and throw it into the water.

2. Action intimately connected with that of the verb which follows it, either as *medial to* its accomplishment or as *the mode of* its acomplishment.

Ex. તે માહારી શાથે દગો કરીને ચાલેછે He deals deceitfully with me.

3. When the action which it denotes, is not physical but relates to exercises of mind, it expresses that action as contemporaneous with or as prior to the action of the conjoined verb, as may depend on the nature of the mental exercise.

Ex. ઈશ્વરની બીહીક રાખીને ચાલો Walk *fearing* God.

The imperfect form even when expressing physical action is chiefly limited in its power to that of medial or modal action.

Ex. લખી જણાવું છઉં I make known by writing.

This participle is, like the others, repeated to denote repeated action.

Future Part. લખવાનો to, about to, going to, write—is declinable. This is of the same form as the genitive of the gerund, but is not to be confounded with it. It signifies action to take place in future time. Whenever used, the auxiliary is expressed or understood.

Ex. હું કંઈ કેહેવાનો છઉં I *am going to say* something.

This participle, although seeming to express intention of mind, &c. does not really do so; it merely expresses futurity.

Participial Noun. લખનાર writer—is formed by adding નાર to the root. It is declinable. It denotes simply and solely a thing or person in whom the action of the verb resides. It is no tense, i. e. it expresses no manner of time, as is supposed by some. By expressing the action of the verb as inherent in an individual, it affords the strongest inference that such action will take place, but it of itself does not express this. This is especially the case in a negative proposition, where by denying the residence of the action, it is assumed that the action never will take place.

હું એવું કામ કરનાર નથી I am not the doer of such a thing. (I will or would never do such a thing).

This noun is therefore a perfect equivalent to the English participial noun in *er*, or the Latin in *or*. It is often used, however, when the English uses the present to express general quality.

Ex. વાઘ માશ ખાનાર છે The tiger eats flesh, (is an eater of flesh).

Indicative Mood.

Present. લખું છું I write, am writing—is formed by adding છું I am, to the present of the Contingent. It comprehends the power of the English present and expresses

1. Present progressing action.

Ex. હું ચોપડી વાંચું છું I *am reading* a book.

2. Action belonging to universal time; it is therefore used in all general propositions.

3. In familiar conversation, action as about to take place immediately.

હું તમારી સાથે ચાકરને મોકલું છું I am sending (going to send) a servant with you.

4. Action originating in past time, and not yet completed, where the English uses the perfect of the auxiliary.

Ex. તમે કેટલા દાહાડા ગુજરાતી ભણોછો How long have you been studying Gujaráti? (do you study).

5. It is used in narrative of past events, when writing seriatim.

6. It expresses future action, which on account of its certainty, is viewed as present, by the speaker.

Ex. આ વરશ હું મુંબાઈ જાઉં છુઉં I *go* (shall go) this year to Bombay.

Imperfect. હું લખતો હતો I was writing, wrote—consists of the present participle and હતો, was. Both elements are declinable. It signifies

1. Past progressive action.

Ex. હું માહારૂં ઘર બાંધતો હતો I *was building* my house.

2. Habitual past action.

Ex. અંગરેજો પેહેલાં મુરતીઓને પુજતા હતા The English formerly *worshipped* idols.

This use is very frequent, and naturally issues from the first, inasmuch as past progressive action indefinitely continued, is customary past action. Here, the Present and Imperfect correspond in their respective powers, each expressing both action progressing and action habitual.

The auxiliary હતો is sometimes omitted, especially if the tense be repeated twice or thrice, when it follows the last.

Ex. તે ધમકાવતો ને મશકરી કરતો હતો He was scolding and mocking.

Aorist Trans. મે લખ્યું I wrote, have written.

Intransitive. હું બોલ્યો I said, have said—is formed by suffixing ય and a gendral suffix to the root. It is identical with the past Gerund in point of time, being entirely indefinite, signifying no more than the English participles said, gone, come, &c. Whether the time be remote or proximate, can be deduced only from the circumstance of use. It can be rendered definite only by the auxiliary. The English Aorist and Perfect are both needed to express its power. It is used

1. in all narrative, expressing sequence of action, as the English Aorist, save when customary action, or action taking place independently in a definite portion of time, is expressed.

2. In conversation as the English perfect, to express action as having now taken place.

Ex. શરકારે એવો હુકુમ આપ્યો કે The Government has given an order, that &c.

Perfect. Trans. મે લખ્યું છે I have written.

Intrans. હું બોલ્યો છુઞ I have said. This tense denotes finished action in past time, conceived of as coming down to the present moment. It is an exact equivalent to the English perfect.

Ex. મે તેના ઊપર કાગલ લખ્યો છે I have written a letter to (on) him.

Remote Perfect. Trans. મે લખેલું છે I have written.

Intrans. હું બોલેલો છુઞ I have said—expresses past remoteness.

Ex. હું ઘણા દાહાડા વીદીયા ભણેલો છુઞ I have learned science for a long time.

Pluperfect Trans. મે લખ્યું હતું I wrote, had written.

Intrans. હું બોલ્યો હતો I said, had said. This tense refers the finished action of indefinite time of the aorist, to the remote past, i. e. to time recognized as past relatively to some other time, and this circumstance renders the time definite. Whereas the perfect brings down the indefinite to a precise point in *present* time, this tense throws it back into a precise point in *past* time. When expressing action in past time unconnected with other action, it is rendered by the English aorist.

Ex. 1. શીકંદર હીંદુસ્થાનમાં આવ્યો હતો Alexander *came* into Hindústán.

2. મે તમને કદી જોયા નોહોતા I never *saw* you.

When expressing action past relatively to other action, it is rendered by the English pluperfect.

Ex. તે માહારે હીયાં આવ્યો તે વારે હું ગયો હતો I *had gone*, when he came to my house.

Remote Pluperfect—differs from the above only in the circumstance of time.

Ex. તે દાહાડાને પેહેલાં મે કાગલ લખેલા હતા I had written a letter before that day.

First Future હું લખીશ I will, or shall write, is formed by suffixing ઈશ to the root.

1. It comprehends the English future.

2. It is used frequently where the English uses should, or would, expressing action *viewed* as further.

Fx. જો હું મરીશ તો મને દાટજો If I die, or should die, bury me.

3. Where the English uses the present, especially when headed by જેવારે.

Ex. જેવારે માહારો ભાઈ આવશે &c. When my brother comes.

4. It expresses potential can, should.

Ex. તે માસ શી રીતે ખાશે? How can, or how should he eat meat?

Observe. This last use does not express abstract capacity but ability under supposed future circumstances. This tense is used as a strong imperative.

Ex. તમે તાંહાં જશો નહી Do not, i. e. you must not, go there.

The above uses of the Future are purely philosophical, as they all denote action viewed as future.

1st. Future 2nd form. હું લખતો હોઈશ I shall be writing. See the power of હોઈશ, and mode of distinguishing it from the contingent.

Ex. આવતી કાલે દશ વાગતે હું લખતો હોઈશ I shall be writing at 10 o'clock to morrow.

2nd. Future. હું લખવાનો છઉં I am to, am going to, write. This tense expresses action *to* take place in the future, with express reference to the present whence that action is to issue.

Ex. હું લખતાં શીખવાનો છઉં I am going to learn to write.

3rd. Future. હું લખવાનો હતો I was to, was going to, write. This tense denotes action *to* take place in past time, i. e. action issuing out of a past moment into future time.

Ex. હું શીખવાનો હતો પણ I was going to learn, but &c.

Observe. Owing to the different idioms of the English and Gujaráti whereby narrative, speech, thought, &c. are represented in the one, under persons and tenses, which are not used in the other, the rendering oft enses will be often found to differ ; e. g. the present will be used for the imperfect, &c. (see Syntax).

Observe. The future perfect is wanting. Its place is occupied by the verb in a compound state with રહેવું to remain, which signifies finished action. (See Compound Verbs).

Contingent Mood.

This Mood demands the special attention of the student. It expresses contingent action, i. e. action viewed as dependent for its taking place on external circumstances, or on the intention of the mind.

It is in this Grammar called the Contingent Mood, inasmuch as it comprehends the contingent uses of the English Potential,* Conditional, and Subjunctive† Moods, which have no appropriate form in Gujaráti. The same form may, under different circumstances of use and different relationships in a sentence, have respectively the signification of all the above moods. To present distinct moods would therefore mislead the student.

The power of the Subjunctive is possessed by the verb in this mood only when governed by an hypothetical conjunction. The power of the Potential, inclusive of the conditional, is possessed by the verb when it is contained either in an independent sentence (interrogative or declarative), or in a dependent clause of a hypothetical sentence. Such clause may either precede or succeed the sentence on which it is dependent, or that sentence may be understood. In either case, there is a dependence which is expressed by this mood as emphatically as though there were an appropriate mood.

The Optative sense is not inherent in this mood, but it may be expressed by the Subjunctive with a dependent sentence expressing desire, hope, &c.

---

* From the potential are excluded the ideas of inherent capacity and obligation. These ideas cannot be expressed by this mood but by other appropriate verbs. Ability is expressed by the passive verb (see Passive).

† By Subjunctive understand the Indicative made hypothetical (see Murray's Grammar).

Would that he were here, is rendered by જો તે હીયાં હોત તો શારૂં.

May he perish, by તે નાશ થાઅે તો શારૂં

God grant that his *son may live long*, by પરમેશ્વર કરેને તેનો દીકરો જીવે.

As this mood expresses the same modification of time as the Indicative, (the tenses of the one corresponding to those of the other,) and therefore differs from it only in the fact of *contingency*, specific remarks as to time under each tense are unncessary. Illustrations serve every purpose.

Contingent 1st Present. હું લખું I may, &c. write. This tense in its multiplied powers comprehends all the other contingent tenses, save in the single circumstance of time; so that in reality, with this exception, no other is needed to express all the modifications of contingency of the whole mood.

This single tense may therefore be represented by every symbol of the English Subjunctive, Potential, and Conditional moods, save in the circumstance of time. It expresses

1. The mere Subjunctive differing only from the Indicative present in the fact of its *not* being declarative but hypothetical. This is a frequent use.

Ex. જો તે છોકરાને મારે તો મને કેહેજો If he *beat* the boy, tell me.

2. This tense expresses the intention of mind, as is represented by the English "*will*" and first person "*shall.*"

Ex. જો તમારી ઇછા હોઅે તો હું તમારી શાથે ફરૂં If you like I *will* take a walk with you.

3. This tense expresses the peculiar contingency involved in the *nature of things*—the character of agents,—the force of circumstance, and also logical and circumstantial inference—such as are represented in English by will or would, can or could,

may or might, *when used without reference to time or inherent capacity of the agent.*

Ex. 1. ખ્રીસટી માણશ જુંઠું કદી ન બોલે A Christian *would* or *will* never tell a lie.

Ex. 2. કીડી હાતીને કેમ મારે? How *could* an ant kill an elephant?

Ex. 3. કીડી હાતીને મારે તો તે વાઘને પણ મારે If an ant can (or could) kill an elephant, it *can* or *could* or *might* also kill a tiger.

Ex. 4. વરસાદ આવે તો અનાજ ઘણો પાકે If rain comes, much grain *will* ripen.

4. This tense is used to express a purpose or end, when it is governed by a conjugation, either preceding or succeeding expressive of finality, as કે that એ માટે therefore, in order to. In such a case it is rendered in English by *may, might, should, or by the infinitive of the verb.*

Ex. 1. તે શુધરે માટે મે તેને શીખામણ દીધી I punished him in order that he *might* improve.

Ex. 2. રાત્રે માણસને અજવાળું થાએ માટે ચંદ્ર પ્રકાશ કરેછે The moon shines that men *may* have light at night.

It sometimes happens that instead of using the conjunction expressing finality, the sentence is placed in an independent form, and made to appear as the subject of a proposition.

Ex. શું તે મને ગાળો દે તે તમને સારૂં લાગેછે? Does it seem to you good that he *should abuse* me (or for him to abuse me)?

5. This tense is used, with the above English rendering in an independent sentence, to express a supposition, a something granted or allowed.

Ex. 1. એક વખત તે ચુક કરે પણ He *may* (or might) make a mistake once, but &c.

Ex. 2. તે વીસ ગાઊ લગી ચાલે પણ He *may* (or might) *walk* twenty gáú, but &c.

6. This tense is used in interrogative sentences to express that slight incumbency to action, or opportuneness of action, which is represented by the English *should*, *shall*, *must*, or by the substantive verb followed by the infinitive, as in the phrase, What am I now to to do?

Ex. 1. હું માહારો પુરવેનો ધરમ શા વાશતે મુકી દેઉં ? Why *should* I leave my ancient religion?

2. માહારો છોકરો મરી ગયો હવે હું શું કરૂં My child is dead, what *shall I* now *do?* (or can).

3. શું દાણા છતાં હમે ભુખે મરી જઇએ *Must we die* of hunger whilst there is grain?

7. This tense expresses habitual action, such as is rendered by the English "will."

Ex. તે રોજ રોજ જંગલમાં જાએ ને આખો દાહાડો રડે He *will* go daily into the jungle and *will* then weep all the day.

When relating to past events, this of course must be rendered by "would."

Ex. તે વીલાતમાં હતો તેઆરે તે નીત દુકાનો જોતો ફરે When he was in Europe, he *would go* about every day looking at the shops.

8. When used in an interrogative sentence in the first person it is used to make a proposal, or ask permission, as is rendered in English by shall, may,

Ex. 1. હું જાઉં *May* I go?

2. હું તેને તમારો હુકમ કહું? *Shall* I give him your orders?

2nd. Present. હું લખતો હોઉં I may, &c. be writing. For the power of this tense, see the power of the auxiliary હોઉં page 62 which is of course equivalent, and which is expressed by be, must, can, could, may, let, and in a reiterative sentence, by the indicative. Let the following illustrations be studied.

1. and 2. જો તે મુંબઈમાં રેહેતો હોએ તો તેહેની વહુ પણ રેહેતી હોએ If he *be* living in Bombay, (sub.) 2. His wife *must* also be living there.

3. તે એવા ખોટા શેહેરમાં રેહેતો નહોએ He *cannot* be living in so wicked a city.

4. તે તાંહાં રેહેતો હોએ પણ હું શું કરવા રહું He *may* be living there, but why should I live there?

5. જો રેહેતો હોએ તો રેહેતો હોએ ને જો જતો હોએ તો જતો હોએ હું કંઈ કેહેનાર નથી If he be stopping *let him stop*, and if he be going *let him go*, I shall not say any thing.

6. જે ઉતરતું હોએ તે ઉતરતું હોએ ને જે ચડતું હોએ તે ચડતું હોએ &c. What is descending *is* descending, and what is rising *is* rising &c.

7. હું એવા મુરખ લોકોમાં કેમ રેહેતો હોઉં? *Why should I be living* amongst so foolish a people?

This species of sentence very commonly has the force of the third use given above.

3rd. Present (dubitative). હું લખતો હોઈશ I be, may be, writing. This differs from the second present, in the same way as હોઈશ differs from હોઉં viz. the action of the former is purely hypothetical; whereas that of the latter is viewed as contingent in circumstance.

Ex. 1. and 2. જો તે ધંધો કરતો હોશે તો તે પઈસા પેદા કરતો હોશે If he *be* working, he *may be* getting money.

Aorist. હું લખત I were to, should, would, write, have written. This is the conditional. Strictly speaking, this has no reference to time, save that it precludes the idea of action having yet taken place. See the power of હોત page 64, which corresponds, save in the circumstance of conditionality.

Ex. 1. જો આપણો રાજા મરત If our king *were to die.*

2. તો આપણાપર કેહેવી સંકટ પડત Then, how much evil *would* ensue to us.

3. (conditional). જો તે મને શીખવત તો હું શીખત If he would teach me, *I would learn.*

4. શું છોકરો પોતાના બાપને મારત? ન મારત What! *could* the child *have killed* his father? He could not have killed.

5. છોકરો પોતાના બાપને મારત ખરો પણ પોતાની માને તે કેમ મારત? The child might indeed have killed his father, but how *could he have killed* his mother?

Observe. 6. This is likewise a pluperfect when it denotes action dependent on the will. As the proper pluperfect લખ્યું હોત precludes from the nature of the auxiliary which can only express pure existenc, the idea of volition, desire, &c. this is used in its stead.

Ex. જો તમે તેની પાશે માગ્યું હોત તો તે તમને જીવતું પાણી આપત If you had asked of him, he *would have given* you living water.

In this example, as the speaker probably signified his own willingness to give, and not the simple fact that such would have been the case, this tense is required in the latter clause, but only on such conditionality.

Aorist 2nd Form. હું લખતો હોત I were, would, should, could, might be, writing. See the power of હોત page 64, which exactly corresponds.

Ex. 1. જો તે ભણતો હોત If he *were studying.*

2. તો તે પોતાનું સારૂં કરતો હોત *He would be doing* himself good.

3. તે વખતે તે ગુજરાતમાં કેમ રેહેતો હોત How *could he be living* at that time in Gujarát?

4. તે તાંહાંથી જતો હોત પણ &c. He *might indeed be going*, or *have been going* thence, but &c.

Perfect Trans. મે લખ્યું હોય્મે I have, may, must, can, could have written. Intrans. હું બોલ્યો હોઊં I have, may, &c. have said. See the power of હોઊં.

Ex. 1. જો તે તાંહાં ગયો હોય્મે If he *have gone* there.

2. તો તેણે પોતાનું વતન મુક્યું હોય્મે Then he *must have left* his native place.

3. તેણે એ કામ કદી કરૂં નહોય્મે He *can* never *have committed* such an action.

4. તેણે એક વખત ઠોકર ખાધી હોય્મે તે વલી ઠોકર કેમ ખાય્મે He *may have stumbled* once (granted), but how can he stumble a second time?

5. It is used in a reiterative sense, where the English uses the present. See 6th use of હોય્મે.

Ex. એને મલ્યું હોય્મે તો મલ્યું હોય્મે મને નહી મલ્યું If he has obtained it, he *has*, but I have not.

Perfect 2nd Form. (dubitative) Trans. મે લખ્યું હોશે I have, I may have, written. Intrans. હું બોલ્યો હોઈશ I have, may have, said. See wherein હોયે and હોસે differ.

Ex. 1. જો તેણે ભુંડું કામ કરૂં હોશે If he *have done* an evil action.

2. તો તે સજા પામ્યો હોશે He *may have* received punishment.

Pluperfect Trans. મે લખ્યું હોત I had, would, should, could, might have, written. Intrans. હું બોલ્યો હોત I had, would, &c. have said. See the power of હોત page 64.

Ex. 1. જો વરસાદ વર્શો હોત If rain *had come*.

2. તો ઘણું અનાજ પાક્યું હોત Much grain *would have ripened*.

3. તેણે એવો હુકમ કર્યો નહોત He *could* never *have given* such an order.

4. તેણે એવી આજ્ઞા આપી હોત પણ તમારે પાલવી નોહોતી He *might* indeed *have given* such a command, but you ought not to have obeyed.

1st Future (present). હું લખવાનો હોઊં I be, may, must, can, could, be about to write. See power of હોઊં page 62.

Ex. 1. જો તે ગાદીપર બેશવાનો હોય્મે If *he be about to sit* on the throne.

2. તો જે હમણાં બેઠોછે તે મુકવાનો હોએ Then, who is now seated, *must be about to leave it.*

3. એવો શારો ચાકર માહારી ચાકરી કેમ મુકવાનો હોએ? How *can* so good a servant *be about to leave* my service?

4. તે માહારૂ ભુંડું કરવાનો હોએ ખરો પણ માહારાથી તેનું ભુંડું કેમ કરાએ He *may* indeed *be about to do evil* to me (granted), but how can I do him evil?

2nd Future (dubitative). હું લખવાનો હોઈશ I be, may be about to write. See the difference between હોઉં and હોઈશ.

Ex. 1. જો તે લડવાનો હોશે If he *be about to fight.*

2. તો તેનો શતરૂ પણ લડવાનો હોશે His enemy also *may be about to fight.*

3rd Future (past). હું લખવાનો હોત I were, should, would, could, might be, have been, about to write.

Ex. 1. જો તે જવાનો હોત If he *were about to go.*

2. તો તેને બદલે બીજો આવવાનો હોત Another *would be about to come in in his stead.*

3. તે એવું કામ કરવાનો કેમ હોત How *could he have been about to do* such an action.

4. તે હીયાં આવવાનો હોત પણ &c. He *might* indeed *have been about to come,* but &c.

Add to the above compound tenses, Rem. Perfect લખેલો હોઉં, લખેલો હોઈશ, and Rem. Pluerfect લખેલો હોત. These need no illustrations, as they correspond to the Perfect tenses in every thing, save the circumstance of time.

CONJUGATION OF THE INTRANSITIVE VERB થા BE,* BECOME, &c.

Imperative Mood.

થા. *(Root).*

PRESENT.

Singular.	*Plural.*
થા be thou.	થા ઓ be ye.

FUTURE.

થજે or થાજે be thou.	થજો or થાજો be ye.

Infinitive Mood.

	m.	*f.*	*n.*	
Sing.	થવો	વી	વું	to be, &c.
Plur.	થવા	વી	વાં	

Present Gerund.	*Past Gerund.*
Nom. & Ac. થવું the being.	*Nom. & Ac.* થયું the having been.
Gen. (*m.* *f.* *n.*) થવાનો ની નું of the being.	*Gen.* (*m* *f* *n*) થઆનો ની નું of the having been.
Dat. થવાને (supine) to be (final).	*Dat.* થયાને to the having been.

(Declinable with other Prepositions).

---

* The word "be" is any thing but a corresponding word, but it is employed as a facile rendering. *Become* and *get* are frequently used as થા.

Participles.

	1st. Present.				*2nd. Present.*
	m.	*f.*	*n.*		(Indeclinable).
Sing.	થતો	તી	તું	being.	થતાં being.
Plur.	થતા	તી	તાં		

	Past.				*Comp. Past.*
Sing.	થયેલો	લી	લું	been.	થઈ or થઈને *Having been.*
Plur.	થયેલા	લી	લાં		

FUTURE.

	m.	*f.*	*n.*	
Sing.	થવાનો	ની	નું	about to be.
Plur.	થવાના	ની	નાં	

ORIGINAL PART. NOUN.

Part. Noun. થનાર be-er.

GENERAL FORMS DECLINABLE.

Singular.				*Plural.*		
m.	*f.*	*n.*		*m.*	*f.*	*n.*
થનારો	રી	રૂં.	|	થનારાઓ	રી	રાં.

Indicative Mood.

PRESENT TENSE.

Am being, &c.

m. *f.* *n.*

Singular.		*Plural.*	
હું થાઉંછઉં	I am being.	હમે થાઈએ-છઈએ	we are being.
તું થાએછે	thou art being.	તમે થાઓછો	you are being.
તે થાએછે	he is being.	તેઓ થાએછે	they are being.

Imperfect.

(Declinable).

Was being, &c.

Singular.		*Plural.*	
હું થતો હતો	I was being.	હમે થતા હતા	we were being.
તું થતો હતો	thou wast being.	તમે થતા હતા	you were being.
તે થતો હતો	he was being.	તેઓ થતા હતા	they were being.

Aorist.

Was, have been.

Singular. m.	f.	n.		*Plural.* m.	f.	n.	
હું થયો	થઈ	થયું	I was, &c.	હમે થયા	થઈ	થયાં	were, &c.
તું થયો	થઈ	થયું	thou wast, &c.	તમે થયા	થઈ	થયાં	you were, &c.
તે થયો	થઈ	થયું	he was, &c.	તેઓ થયા	થઈ	થયાં	they were, &c.

Perfect.

(Declinable).

Have been.

Singular.		*Plural.*	
હું થયો છઉં	I have been.	હમે થયા છઈએ	we have been.
તું થયો છે	thou hast been.	તમે થયા છો	you have been.
તે થયો છે	he has been.	તેઓ થયા છે	they have been.

Remote Perfect.

(Declinable).

Have been.

Singular.		*Plural.*	
હું થયેલો છઉં	I have been.	હમે થયેલા છઈએ	we have been.

Conjugated as the perfect.

PLUPERFECT.

(Declinable).

Was. Had been.

Singular.		*Plural.*	
હું થયો હતો	I had been.	હમે થયા હતા	we had been.
તું થયો હતો	thou hadst been.	તમે થયા હતા	you had been.
તે થયો હતો	he had been.	તેઓ થયા હતા	they had been.

REM. PLUPERFECT.

(Declinable).

Singnlar.		*Plural.*	
હું થયેલો હતો	I had been.	હમે થયેલા હતા	we had been.

Conjugated as the pluperfect.

FUTURE.

m. f. n.

Will, shall be.

Singular.		*Plural.*	
હું થઇશ	I will be.	હમે થઇશું શ	we will be.
તું થશે	thou wilt be.	તમે થશો	you will be.
તે થશે	he will be.	તેઓ થશે	they will be.

2ND. FORM.

(Declinable).

Will, shall be, being.

Singular.			*Plural.*		
હું થતો હોઇશ	I will be,	being.	હમે થતા હોઇશું	we will be,	being.
તું થતો હોશે	thou wilt be,		તમે થતા હોશો	you will be,	
તે થતો હોશે	he will be,		તેઓ થતા હોશે	they willbe,	

2ND. FUTURE (PRESENT).

(Declinable).

Am about to be.

Singular.		*Plural.*	
હું થવાનો છુંજ	I am, &c.	હમે થવાના છુઈએ	we are, &c.
તું થવાનો છે	thou art, &c.	તમે થવાના છો	you are, &c.
તે થવાનો છે	he is, &c.	તેઓ થવાના છે	they are, &c.

3RD. FUTURE. (PAST).

(Declinable).

Was about to be.

Singular.		*Plural.*	
હું થવાનો હતો	I was, &c.	હમે થવાના હતા	we were, &c.
તું થવાનો હતો	thou wast, &c.	તમે થવાના હતા	you were, &c.
તે થવાનો હતો	he was, &c.	તેઓ થવાના હતા	they were, &c

Contingent Mood.

1ST. PRESENT TENSE.

m. f. n.

Be, may and can be.

Singular.		*Plural.*	
હું થાઉં	I be, &c.	હમે થાઈએ	we be.
તું થાએ	thou be'est.	તમે થાઓ	you be.
તે થાએ	he be.	તેઓ થાએ	they be.

2ND. PRESENT.

(Declinable).

Be, may be, &c. being.

Singular.		*Plural.*	
હું થતો હોઉં	I be, being.	હમે થતા હોઈએ	we be, being.
તું થતો હોએ	thou be'est, being.	તમે થતા હોઓ	you be, being.
તે થતો હોએ	he be, being.	તેઓ થતા હોએ	they be, being.

3rd Present. (Dubitative).

(Declinable).

Be, may be, being.

Singular.		*Plural.*	
હું થતો હોઇશ	I be, being.	હમે થતા હોઇશું	we be, being.

Conjugated as the Future Indicative.

Aorist.

m. f. n.

Were to be, would, &c. be.

Singular.		*Plural.*	
હું થાત	I would, &c. be.	હમે થાત	we would be.
તું થાત	thou would'st be.	તમે થાત	you would be.
તે થાત	he would be.	તેઓ થાત	they would be.

2nd Form.

(Declinable).

Were being, would, &c. be being.

Singular.		*Plural.*	
હું થતો હોત	I were being, &c.	હમે થતા હોત	we were being, &c.
તું થતો હોત	thou wert being, &c.	તમે થતા હોત	you were being, &c.
તે થતો હોત	he were being, &c.	તેઓ થતા હોત	they were being, &c.

Perfect.

(Declinable).

Have been, may, &c. have been.

Singular.		*Plural.*	
હું થયો હોઉં	I may, &c.	હમે થયા હોઇએ	we may, &c.
તું થયો હોએ	thou may'st, &c.	તમે થયા હોઓ	you may, &c.
તે થયો હોએ	he may, &c.	તેઓ થયા હોએ	they may, &c.

2ND FORM. (DUBITATIVE).

(Declinable).

Have, may have been.

Singular.		Plural.	
હું થયો હોઈશ	I may, &c.	હમે થયા હોઈશ-શું	we may, &c.
તું થયો હોશે	thou may'st, &c.	તમે થયા હોશો	you may, &c.
તે થયો હોશે	he may, &c.	તેઓ થયા હોશે	they may, &c.

PLUPERFECT.

(Declinable).

Had been, would, &c. have been.

Singular.		Plural.	
હું થયો હોત	I would, &c.	હમે થયા હોત	we would, &c.
તું થયો હોત	thou would'st, &c.	તમે થયા હોત	ye would, &c.
તે થયો હોત	he would, &c.	તેઓ થયા હોત	they would, &c.

1ST FUTURE. (PRESENT).

(Declinable).

Be, &c. about to be.

Singular.		Plural,	
હું થવાનો હોઉં	I be, &c.	હમે થવાના હોઈએ	we be, &c.
તું થવાનો હોએ	thou be'est, &c.	તમે થવાના હોઓ	ye be, &c.
તે થવાનો હોએ	he be, &c.	તેઓ થવાના હોએ	they be, &c.

2ND FUTURE. (DUBITATIVE).

(Declinable).

Be, may be, about to be.

Singular		Plural.	
હું થવાનો હોઈશ	I may be, &c.	હમે થવાના હોઈશું	we may be, &c.
તું થવાનો હોશે	thou may'st be, &c.	તમે થવાના હોશો	you may be, &c.
તે થવાનો હોશે	he may be, &c.	તેઓ થવાના હોશે	they may be, &c.

3RD FUTURE. (PAST.)

(Declinable).

Were, would, &c. be, about to be.

Singular.		*Plural.*	
હું થવાનો હોત	I would be, &c.	હમે થવાના હોત	we would be, &c.
તું થવાનો હોત	thou would'st be, &c.	તમે થવાના હોત	you would be, &c.
તે થવાનો હોત	he would be &c.	તેઓ થવાના હોત	they would be, &c.

NEGATIVE FORMS OF TENSES.

(Declinable).

Imperative.	તું ન થતો તું થતો મા	Be thou not.
Present.	હું થતો નથી	I am not being.
Imp.	હું થતો નોહોતો	I was not being.
Perfect.	હું થયો નથી	I have not been.
Remote Perf.	હું થએલો નથી	I have not been.
Pluperfect.	હું થયો નોહોતો	I had not been.
Rem. Pluperf.	હું થએલો નોહોતો	I had not been.

The auxiliary forms may be placed before the verb, as હું નોહોતો થયો.

CONJUGATION OF THE TRANSITIVE VERB* લખ WRITE.

Imperative Mood.

લખ *(Root of the verb).*

PRESENT.

Singular.	*Plural.*
2nd. P. લખ write thou.	લખો write ye.

* For the exact rendering of each tense see Remarks.

FUTURE.

2nd. P. લખજે write thou. | લખજો write ye.

Infinitive Mood and Gerunds.

	m.	*f.*	*n.*	
Sing.	લખવો	વી	વું	to write.
Plur.	લખવા	વી	વાં	

Present Gerund.	*Past Gerund.*
Nom. & Ac. લખવું the writing.	*Nom & Ac.* લખ્યું the having written.
Gen. લખવાનો ની નું of the writing.	*Gen.* લખ્યાનો ની નું of the having written.
Dat. લખવાને to the writing or (supine) to write (final).	*Dat.* લખ્યાને to the having written.

Declinable with other prepositions.

PARTICIPLES.

1st. Present.					*2nd. Present.*	*Past.*				
	m.	*f.*	*n.*				*m.*	*f.*	*n.*	
Sing.	લખતો	તી	તું	writing	લખતાં.	*Sing.*	લખેલો	લી	લું	written.
Plur.	લખતા	તી	તાં			*Plur.*	લખેલા	લી	લાં	

Compound Past. લખી or લખીને having written.

FUTURE.

	m.	*f.*	*n.*	
Sing.	લખવાનો	ની	નું	about to write.
Plur.	લખવાના	ની	નાં	

Partl. Noun. લખનાર writer.

General Forms.

(Declinable).

	m.	f.	n.
Sing.	લખનારો	રી	રૂં
Plur.	લખનારાઓ	રી	રાં

Indicative Mood.

Present Tense.

Write, am writing.

Singular.		*Plural.*	
હું લખું છુજ	I write, &c.	હમે લખીએ છુઈએ	we write, &c.
તું લખેછે	thou writest.	તમે લખોછો	you write.
તે લખેછે	he writes.	તેઓ લખેછે	they write.

Imperfect.

(Declinable).

Was writing, did write.

Singular.		*Plural.*	
હું લખતો હતો	I was writing.	હમે લખતા હતા	we were writing.
તું લખતો હતો	thou wast writing.	તમે લખતા હતા	you were writing.
તે લખતો હતો	he was writing.	તેઓ લખતા હતા	they were writing.

Aorist.

(Declinable).

Wrote, have written.

Singular.		*Plural.*	
મે લખ્યું	I wrote.	હમે લખ્યું	we wrote.
તેં લખ્યું	thou wrotest.	તમે લખ્યું	you wrote.
તેણે લખ્યું	he wrote.	તેઓએ લખ્યું	they wrote.

PERFECT.

(Declinable).

Have written.

Singular.		*Plural.*	
મેં લખ્યુંછે	I have written.	હમે લખ્યુંછે	we have written.
તેં લખ્યુંછે	thou hast written.	તમે લખ્યુંછે	you have written.
તેણે લખ્યુંછે	he has written.	તેઓએ લખ્યુંછે	they have written.

REMOTE PERFECT.

(Declinable).

Singular.		*Plural.*	
મે લખેલું છે	I have written.	હમેલખેલું છે	we have written,

Conjugated as perfect.

PLUPERFECT.

(Declinable).

Wrote had written.

Singular.		*Plural.*	
મે લખ્યું હતું	I had written.	હમે લખ્યું હતું	we had written.
તેં લખ્યું હતું	thou hadst written.	તમે લખ્યું હતું	you had written.
તેણે લખ્યું હતું	he had written.	તેઓએ લખ્યું હતું	they had written.

REMOTE PLUPERFECT.

(Declinable).

Singular.		*Plural.*	
મેં લખેલુ હતું	I had written.	હમે લખેલુ હતું	we had written.

Conjugated as the pluperfect.

1st Future.

m. f. n.

Will, shall, write.

Singular.		*Plural.*	
હું લખીશ	I will write.	હમે લખીશું-શે	we will write.
તું લખશે	thou wilt write.	તમે લખશો	you will write.
તે લખશે	he will write.	તેઓ લખશે	they will write.

2nd Form.

(Declinable).

હું લખતો હોઇશ I shall be writing.	હમે લખતા હોઇશું we shall be writing; conjugated as the present contingent.

2nd Future (Present).

(Declinable).

About to write.

Singular.		*Plural.*	
હું લખવાનો છુઉં	I am, &c.	હમે લખવાના છુઇએ	we are, &c.
તું લખવાનો છે	thou art, &c.	તમે લખવાના છો	you are, &c.
તે લખવાનો છે	he is, &c.	તેઓ લખવાના છે	they are, &c.

3rd Future (Past).

(Declinable).

About to write.

Singular.		*Plural*	
હું લખવાનો હુતો	I was, &c.	હમે લખવાના હુતા	we were, &c.
તું લખવાનો હુતો	thou wast, &c.	તમે લખવાના હુતા	you were, &c.
તે લખવાનો હુતો	he was, &c.	તેઓ લખવાના હુતા	they were, &c.

Contingent Mood.

1st Presnt.

m. *f.* *n.*

I write, may, can, &c. write.

Singular.		*Plural.*	
હું લખું	I may write.	હમે લખીએ	we may write.
તું લખે	thou may'st write.	તમે લખો	you may write.
તે લખે	he may write.	તેઓ લખે	they may write.

2nd Present.

(Declinable).

Be, may, can, &c. be writing.

Singular.		*Plural.*	
હું લખતો હોઉં	I be writing.	હમે લખતા હોઈએ	we be writing.
તું લખતો હોએ	thou be'est writing.	તમે લખતા હોઓ	you be writing.
તે લખતો હોએ	he be writing.	તેઓ લખતા હોએ	they be writing.

3rd. Present.

(Declinable).

Be, may be, writing.

Singular.		*Plural.*	
હું લખતો હોઈશ	I may be writing.	હમે લખતા હોઈશે-શું	We may be writing.
તું લખતો હોશે	thou may'st be writing.	તમે લખતા હોશો	you may be writing.
તે લખતો હોશે	he may be writing.	તેઓ લખતા હોશે	they may be writing.

Aorist.

m. f. n.

Were to, would, &c. write.

Singular.		*Plural.*	
હું લખત	I would write.	હમે લખત	we would write.
તું લખત	thou would'st write.	તમે લખત	you would write.
તે લખત	he would write.	તેઓ લખત	they would write.

2nd. Form.

(Declinable).

Were, would, &c. be writing.

Singular.		*Plural.*	
હું લખતો હોત	I were writing.	હમે લખતા હોત	we were writing.
તું લખતો હોત	thou wert writing.	તમે લખતા હોત	you were writing.
તે લખતો હોત	he were writing.	તેઓ લખતા હોત	they were writing.

Perfect.

(Declinable).

Have, may, &c. have written.

Singular.		*Plural.*	
મેં લખ્યું હોએ	I may have written.	હમે લખ્યું હોએ	we may have written.
તેં લખ્યું હોએ	thou may'st have written.	તમે લખ્યું હોએ	you may have written.
તેણે લખ્યું હોએ	he may have written.	તેઓએ લખ્યું હોએ	they may have written.

2nd. Form.

(Declinable).

Have, may have, written.

Siugular.		*Plural.*	
મેં લખ્યું હોશે	I may have written.	હમે લખ્યું હોશે	we may have written.
તેં લખ્યું હોશે	thou may'st have written.	તમે લખ્યું હોશે	you may have written.
તેણે લખ્યું હોશે	he may have written.	તેઓએ લખ્યું હોશે	they may have written.

Pluperfect.

(Declinable).

Had, would, &c. have written.

Singular.		*Plural.*	
મેં લખ્યું હોત	I would have written, &c.	હમે લખ્યું હોત	we would have written, &c.
તેં લખ્યું હોત	thou would'st have written, &c.	તમે લખ્યું હોત	you would have written, &c.
તેણે લખ્યું હોત	he would have written, &c.	તેઓએ લખ્યું હોત	they would have written.

1st. Future Present.

(Declinable).

Be, may, &c. be about to write.

Singular:		*Plural.*	
હું લખવાનો હોઉં	I may be about to write.	હમે લખવાના હોઈએ	we may be about to write.
તું લખવાનો હોએ	thou may'st be about to write.	તમે લખવાના હોઓ	you may be about to write.
તે લખવાનો હોએ	he may be about to write.	તેઓ લખવાના હોએ	they may be about to write.

2ND. FUTURE (DUBITATIVE).

Be, may be, about to write.

Singular.	*Plural.*
હું લખવાનો હોઈશ I may be about to write.	હમે લખવાના હોઈશું we may be about to write.
તું લખવાનો હોઈશ thou may'st be about to write.	તમે લખવાના હોશો you may be about to write.
તે લખવાનો હોશે he may be about to write.	તેઓ લખવાના હોશે they may be about to write.

3RD. FUTURE (PAST).

Were, would, &c. be about to write.

Singular.	*Plural.*
હું લખવાનો હોત I were about to write.	હમે લખવાના હોત we were about to write.
તું લખવાનો હોત thou wert about to write.	તમે લખવાના હોત you were about to write.
તે લખવાનો હોત he were about to write.	તેઓ લખવાના હોત they were about to write.

Add to the above the two Remote Perfects and Pluperfects, corresponding to the Indicative.

Negative forms of Tenses.

Present.	હું લખતો નથી	I do not write.
Imperfect.	હું લખતો નોહોતો	I did not write, was not writing.
Perfect.	મે લખ્યું નથી	I have not written.
Rem. Perfect.	મે લખેલું નથી	I have not written.
Pluperfect.	મે લખ્યું નોહોતું	I had not written.
Rem. Pluperf.	મે લખેલું નોહોતું	I had not written.

It has been seen that Intransitive and Transitive Verbs differ in the fact of the former having a real nominative case in all its aorist tenses, and of the latter having a virtual nominative in the ablative case. The intransitive verb થવું has been already conjugated. The student may at once see from the following paradigm the circumstances of difference. Let it be remembered that the tenses having a nominative, are susceptible of change for gender and number as an adjective, e. g. બોલ્યો*m.* બોલી*f.* બોલ્યું*n.*

Aorist.	હું બોલ્યો	I spoke.
Perfect.	હું બોલ્યો છઉં	I have spoken.
Rem. Perfect.	હું બોલેલો છઉં	I have spoken.
Pluperfect.	હું બોલ્યો હતો	I had spoken.
Rem. Pluperf.	હું બોલેલો હતો	I had spoken.
Con. 1. Present.	હું બોલ્યો હોઉં	I may, &c. have spoken.
,, 2. Present.	હું બોલ્યો હોઈશ	I may have spoken.
Pluperfect.	હું બોલ્યો હોત	I would, &c. have spoken.

Add the Remote Perfects and the Remote Pluperfects હું બોલેલો હોઉં. હું બોલેલો હોઈશ. હું બોલેલો હોત.

The following paradigm contains several useful Intransitives.
જમવું and ભાગવું are also Transitives.

સુવું	sleep.	જીવવું	live.
રમવું	play.	મરવું	die.
જમવું	eat.	હસવું	laugh.
બેસવું	sit.	જવું	go.
ચાલવું	walk.	રેહેવું	remain.

દોડવું	run.	ચુકવું	mistake.
જાગવું	awake.	ઊઠવું	arise.
ભણવું	study.	ઊગવું	grow.
શીખવું	learn.	પામવું	receive.
બોલવું	speak.	શકવું	be able.
લાવવું	bring.	ભુલવું	forget.
ભાગવું	break.	વીશરવું	forget.
		મળવું	visit.

The following verbs are Irregular in the formation of the Aorist.

		From their Aorists.	From which are formed the Past Participle, e. g. ગએલો, લીધેલું.
જવું	go.		ગયો
લેવું	take.		લીધું.
દેખવું	see.		દીઠું.
કરવું	do.		કીધું also કર્યું.
મરવું	die.		મુઓ ,, મર્યો.
બેસવું	sit.		બેઠો.
સુવું	sleep.		સુતો
દેવું	give.		દીધું.
નાહાશવું	escape.		નાહાઠો.

1. Verbs whose final letter of a monosyllabic root is ઓ, change the ઓ into ઉ in the formation of the second person plural of the Imperative; e. g. જો see, ધો wash, make જુઓ and ધુઓ; દોહો milk, also frequently makes its second person દુહો. રેહે remain, forms its second person રાહો.

NOTE. The verbs placed in the neuter gender are Transitive, and those placed in the masculine are Intransitive.

2. Monosyllabic roots, having a final આ, drop it in the formation of some few tenses; e. g. જા takes the infinitive form જવું, પા, થવું, &c.

Impersonal Defective Verb conjugated with the pronoun in the dative or ablative case, and declined to agree in gender or number with the object.

Singular.			*Plural.*	
મને or માહારે	જોઇયેછે or	It is needed by me, us, &c.	હમને or હમારે	જોઇયેછે. or
તને or તાહારે	જોઇયેચ or	It is incumbent on me, us, &c.	તમને or તમારે	જોઇયેચ. or
તેને or તેણે	જોઇયે	It is necessary to me, us, &c.	તેઓને or તેઓએ	જોઇયે.

મને *or* માહારે, *&c.*

Indic.	Imperf.	જોઇતું હતું.
,,	Future.	જોઇશે.
Contin.	Present.	જોઇયે.
,,	2nd. Present.	જોઇતું હોયે.
,,	3rd. Present.	જોઇતું હોસે.
,,	Aorist.	જોઇયેત.
,,	2nd. Form.	જોઇતું હોત.

See the Remarks on the pronouns; it will thence be observed that જોઇયે when signifying *ought*, must take the ablative, and when signifying *need*, must take the dative.

Ex. Dat. મને પાંચ રૂપીઆ જોઇયે I want five rupees, (are wanting to me).

2. માહારે શંભાળવું જોઇયે I must, or ought to, take care, (by me it is needful, or on me incumbent).

Passive Verbs.

The mode of forming the Passive Verb is explained in the second part of Etymology.

The conjugation is the same as that of the active verb.

Imperf.	Present.	લખા	be thou written.
„	Future.	લખાજે	be thou written.
Infinit. & Gerund.		લખાવું	to be written, the being written.
Past	Gerund	લખાયું	the having been written.
Present Participle.		લખાતો	written.
Past	Participle.	લખાયેલો	written.
Comp. Part.		લખાઈને	having been written.
Indic.	Present.	હું લખાઉં છઉં	I am written.
	Imperf.	હું લખાતો હતો	I was being written.
	Aorist.	હું લખાયો	I was, have been, written.
	Perfect.	હું લખાયો છઉં	I have been written.
Rem.	Perfect.	હું લખાયેલો છઉં	I have been written.
	Pluperf.	હું લખાયો હતો	I was, had been, written.
Rem.	Pluperf.	હું લખાયેલો હતો	I had been written.
1.	Future.	હું લખાઈશ	I shall be written.
2.	Future.	હું લખાતો હોઈશ	I shall be being written.
Contin.	1. Present.	હું લખાઉં	I be, may, &c. be written.
	2 Prest.	હું લખાતો હોઉં	I may, &c. be being written.
	3. Prest.	હું લખાતો હોઈશ	I may be being written.
	Aorist.	હું લખાત	I would, &c. be written.
	2. Form.	હું લખાતો હોત	I would be being written.
	Perfect.	હું લખાયો હોઉં	I may have been written.

2. Perfect. હું લખાયો હોઇશ I may have been written.

3. Perfect. હું લખાયો હોત I would have been written.

The futures, second and third if required, would be compounded of જવું to go; e. g. લખાઇ જવાનો about to be written.

A few observations on the use of the Passive are here required. The genius of this language is not favourable to its frequent use. Custom has rendered familiar a few verbs in the Passive form in a few tenses. Such verbs are chiefly those which have neuter signification, and do not refer to extrinsic agents. The passiveness of the English verb is, as a general principle, distinct from that of the Gujaráti, which denotes intrinsic condition rather than a condition produced by an extrinsic agent. Hence neuter verbs are converted into Passives rather than active verbs. The following verbs illustrate this remark: પીડા be pained, સુકા be dried, કેહેવા be called. So foreign is the strictly passive verb to the Gujaráti mode of thought, that periphrases, or expressions which to the English seem uncouth, are adopted to avoid its use; e. g. I am beat, is rendered in Gujaráti by હું માર ખાઉં છું I eat (receive) blows. The student will deduce from these remarks the necessity of caution in the use of the passive, and the desirableness of studying the native thought. The passive may generally be superseded by the active verb without an agent expressed. This principle is especially observed with reference to the past participle of verbs active and neuter. See Remarks.

It may here be observed that a substitute occasionally used for the passive is the past Gerund of the active verb, and the verb જવું following it.

Ex. તે મારયો ગયો He was killed.

This mode is very unfrequently used, and does not seem congenial to the language.

It now remains to present to the student the passive verb in its more important use, viz. as a Potential Mood, signifying capability of action. When thus employed, the agent is expressed by the pronoun, &c. in the ablative formed by the preposition થી, and the verb is used either impersonally in the neuter gender, or is made to agree with the object in the nominative.

PASSIVE VERB WITH POTENTIAL SIGNIFICATION.

PRESENT.

I am able to write or by me it is writable.

Singular.		*Plural.*	
માહારાથી	લખાયેછે.	હમારાથી	લખાયેછે.
તાહારાથી		તમારાથી	
તેનાથી		તેઓનાથી	

માહારાથી &c. *By me, thee, &c.*

	Imperf.	લખાતું હતું	it was writable.
	Aoirst.	લખાણું	it was, has been, writable.
	Future.	લખાશે	it will be writable.
Con.	Presnt.	લખાયે	it may, &c. be writable.
	Aorist.	લખાત	it would, &c. be writable.

Add the Compound Tenses.

Illustrations, rendered in idiomatic English.

Ex. 1. જો માહારાથી અવાશે તો હું આવીશ If I *can* come, I will come (if by me it is comeable).

2. તે લંગડો હતો માટે તેનાથી ચલાતું નોહોતું He was lame and therefore could not walk, (by him it was not walkable).

3. શું એ કામ તમારાથી કરાશે ? Will you be able to do this work ? (by you this work be do-able).

Combination of Verbs.

It remains to point out certain modifications of time and action, relatively to the verb which are expressed in this language by the introduction of other verbs. These are as follows:

1. By subjoining the verb જવું with the present participle of the verb, a continuedness of action is expressed.*

Ex. 1. હું લખતો જાઉં છઉં I go on writing.

2. તમે ભણતા જાઓ Go on studying.

2. By subjoining જવું with the past gerund of the verb, remittent action, or continuation of suspended action, such as is expressed in English by "go on with."

Ex. 1. તમે લખ્યા જાઓ Go on with your writing.

2. તે બોલ્યો જાએછે He goes on talking.

3. By subjoining આવવું to come, with the infinitive of another verb, the proximity or the about to be, of the action of that verb is expressed.

Ex. રતુ થવા આવી The season is approaching, (has come to be).

---

* The above use of જવું may be considered as metaphoric. Its literal sense is frequent as well as that of આવવું.

હું કેહેતો ગયો I went saying, (as I went, I said).

હું કેહેતો આવ્યો I came saying, (as I came, I said).

4. By subjoining the same verb to the present participle of another, the continuation of the action of that verb from an indefinite time is expressed.

Ex. હું ભુંડું કરતો આવ્યો I have done evil up to the present (I have come doing evil).

5. By subjoining the verb કરવું to do to the plural neuter of the past Gerund of the verb, frequent action (intermittent) is expressed.

Ex. 1. લખ્યાં કરૂં છુઉં I write frequently.} not remittently.
2. રમ્યાં કરૂં છુઉં I play frequently.}

6. By adding રેહેવું to remain, to the present participle, continuous remittent action is expressed.

Ex. 1. તમે ભણતા રોહોં Be always studying.

2. તમે માહારી પાશે આવતા રોહો Be always coming to me.

7. By using the verb કરવું an attempt at, or commencement of, action is expressed.

Ex. તેણે મારવાનું કરૂં પણ મારૂં નહીં He tried to beat, but he did not beat.

8. For other modifications produced by compounding the past participle, see Etymology 2nd Part. Some of these have been in previous grammars introduced into the regular verb, for the formation of tenses, as લખી રેહીશ for I shall have written. This is erroneous. The above has no more right to be considered a tense of લખ, than I shall finish writing, has to be considered a tense of write. The same remark is applicable to the use of શકવું to express the potential.

Ex. હું ખાઈ શકું છુઉં I can eat.

This is a compound verb, and on no principle a tense of the verb બોલવું.

Preposition.*

Some Prepositions follow the substantive or substantival part of speech in its original or oblique form. Some follow it only when in the genitive case (oblique or in the feminine gender) viz. ના and ની ; others again follow it when placed in the dative ને. The preposition નો of, is declined as follows:

	Singular.				*Plural.*		
	m.	*f.*	*n.*		*m.*	*f.*	*n.*
Nom.	નો	ની	નું.	*Nom.*	ના	ની	નાં
Ob.	ના	ની	ના.	*Ob.*	ના	ની	નાં

Note. This preposition, like the adjective, makes its ablative in એ, instead of આ, when preceding a substantive in the ablative whose ultimate is a consonant with એ, إنصاف

E. G. ઈનસાફને દાહાડે on the day of judgment. †

The following Prepositions generally follow the substantive alone i. e. without its being placed in the genitive.‡

એ by, in, with.

થી, થકી } from, by, with.

માં in.

માંહે within.

શીવાએ besides, except.

ઉપરાંત besides (over and above).

વગર, વીના } without, besides, except.

---

* Many elucidations of the theories of Horne Tooke are to be found in the Gujaráti Preposition and Adverb.

† The ને here is not the dative but merely takes the એ in order to symphonize with the દાહાડે.

‡ The following Classification will be found conformable to general but not to universal, use, which is not uniform.

કરતાં than.

લગી
લગણ
સુધી } up to, as far as.

સમંધી
વીશે } about, respecting.

વડે by, with.

The following Prepositions are post-fixed to the substantive in the genitive feminine ની, as છોકરાંની શાથે with the children.

સાથે
જોડે } with, together.

પછવાડે
પાછળ
પુઠી
પુઠળ } after, behind, backward.

આશપાશ around.

આરપાર across.

બાહાર out, outside.

અગાળી
આગળ
અગાડી } before, in front of.

શાંમુ
શાંમાં
શાંમણે } in front of, opposite, facing.

પાસે
કને } to near.

ગમ
તરફ } towards, to.

નીચે
હેઠે
હેઠળ
તળે } below, under, underneath.

પેઠે like to.

માફક similar to.

હસતક by the hand of.

મારફત through, by medium of.

ભણી. to, towards.

The following are post-fixed to the substantive in the genitive (oblique) ના e. g. છોકરાઓના સુધાં with the children.

સુધાં
સમેત } in conjunction with.

ઊપર above, on.

પર on.

પેહેલાં before (time).

પ્રમાણે like to.

The following are post-fixed to the substantive in the dative case ને; e. g. છોકરાને લીધે on account of the boy.

લીધે	for, on account of.	વતે, બદલે	instead of.	بدل
વાશતે	for, for the sake of.			
સારૂ, કાજે, માટે	for, by cause of, for, in order to.	દોશતે, દોશતી	for the sake of.	دوستی

Add to the above કરીને which is the past participle of કર, but frequently follows the ablative in એ and signifies with, by means of, as હતીઆરે કરીને with an instrument.

Adverbs.

The number of Adverbs, as a distinct part of speech, is very limited.* Such as there are, are not characterized by any peculiar form. To supply the place of adverbs, other parts of speech are used to an indefinite extent in an adverbial sense. 1. The adjective. 2. The preposition simple and compounded. 3. The past participle of the verb. 4. The substantive with a preposition. This latter part of speech in its ablatival form, forms by far the greater part of adverbs. The following illustrations are given of the above principles:

---

* It is evident that the adverbs expressive of mode, may in any language be resolved into a noun and preposition. As, for laboriously, read *with labour;* for emphatically, read *with emphasis.* These two elements may be employed ad libitum in Gujaráti. Hence as many adverbs may be created as there are abstract nouns.

1 Adverbs, whose use is entirely appropriate and which cannot be resolved into other parts of speech.* They are chiefly such as relate to place and time.

હીઆં, હહીં } here.
તાંહાં, તહીં } there.
જાંહાં, જહીં } where.
પહણે, પહીં } there, yonder.
કેમ why?
કાંહાં where?
કાંજે, કાંકે, કેમકે } because.
હાલુ the current year.
હવે now.
હવડાં, હમણાં } now (time).
આજ to day
વળી, વળતી } again.
ફરી, ફરીથી } again, anew.

પોહોર last year.
જટ, જટપટ } quickly.
ઊથલપાથલ, ઊલટપાલટ } topsy turvy.
કદી ever.
તરત soon.
કદાપી, કદાચીત, કદાશ } by any means.
હજુ as yet.
તો yes, surely (also a reflective particle).
જ intensive particle.
છેલાં lastly.
પેહેલાં first.
છેક utterly.
વાઈ well.
એકાંત secretly.
લગભગ closely.
એકાએક, અખશમાત } suddenly.

* Many of the subjoined list if carefully analysed, may be resolved into other parts of speech. It is here meant that they are not used but as adverbs.

કીહ } where, why.
કીત

હો } yes.
હા

હોવે of course.

નો
ના*
નહી } no, not.
નથી
મા

જેમ as.

તેમ so.

એમ thus.

એમનું એમ } in the same way.
તેમનું તેમ

એકમેક all one.

મેલશેલ promiscuously.

2 Adverbs consisting of adjectives either in the nominative or ablative cases :

સાફ plainly.

પ્રગટ } openly.
ઊઘાડું

પ્રથમ first.

અસલ originally.

મોહોડું late.

ઓચીંતું unexpectedly.

છાંનુંમાંનું secretly.

વીશેશ especially.

જરા } a little, somewhat.
જરાક

ઊતાવલે } quickly.
જલદી

ધીરે } slowly.
ધીમે

સાચે } truly.
ખરે

નીધાને At the lowest.

વેગલે at a distance.

એટલે at that time.

નીશ્ચે } certainly.
ખચીત

પુરૂં entirely.

બહુ very.

ઘણું much.

થોડું little.

અતી } very much.
અતીશે

ઠીક correctly.

ઠીકઠાક in right order.

બસ enough.

* This negative, curious to say, is of feminine gender.

3. See illustrations of participles answering the use of adverbs. Add here ઘણું કરીને chiefly, generally.

4. See prepositions, some of which are used adverbially.

5. Substantives duplicated or in ablative case, as follows:

આશરે, શુમારે, અટકળે } about, by guess.
ગણતીએ, જુમલે, સરવાળે } in total amount.
દીશે, દાહાડે } by day.
મહીને by the month.
અઠવાડીએ by the week.
કાલે to morrow, yesterday.
રાતે, રાતરે } at night.
રાતેને રાતે at very night.
શાંજે, શાંજરે } on the evening.
કાંઠે, કીનારે } by the shore of.

મોહોડે, શાંમણે } in front of.
અનુક્રમે in order.
વીગતે, વીગતવારે } seriatim.
વીસતારે at length.
રાતોવાઈ in the night.
રાતની રાત in a night.
વરશો વરશ yearly.
દાહાડે દાહાડે every day.
મહીને મહીને every month.
અઠવાડીએ અઠવાડીએ every week.
રોજ રોજ daily.
વારે વારે frequently.
ઘડી ઘડી hourly.
દમ દમ, પલ પલ } minutely.
શરા શરી on an average.
હારકતાર in rows.

6. In addition to the above may be given an indefinite number of Abstract Nouns with the prepositions એ or થી.

The following are specimens:

મરીઆદાથી respectfully.
બુધીથી wisely.
મુરખાઈથી foolishly.
ચતુરાઈથી skilfully.
જુગતીથી cleverly.
ઉદ્યોગથી industriously.

7. Adjectives duplicated, used as adverbs.

ઓછામાં ઓછું }
થોડામાં થોડું } at the least.

ઘણામાં ઘણું at the most.

શશતામાં શશતું at the cheapest.

&c. &c. &c.

8. Add to the above a few words really a distinct part of speech but clipped so as to appear an adverb, as for જે વારે at which time, જ્યારે when, તે વારે at that time, ત્યારે then. Also adverbs formed by prepositions.

Relatives.	*Correlates.*
જાંહાંસુધી as long as.	તાંહાં સુધી so long as.
જાંહાંથી whence.	તાંહાંથી thence.
જ્યારથી from which time.	ત્યારથી from that time.

And so on by the suffix of other prepositions.

CONJUNCTION.

ને, તથા } and
કે, અથવા } or, whether.
એ, ઓ, પણ } also, but.

કે, જે } that (a connecting particle).

એટલે, that is, viz.

Relative.	*Correlate.*
જો if (hypothetically).	તો then.
જો { પણ if, by assumption. / કદાપી, કદાચ, કદાચીત } if, contingently. }	તોપણ, તથાપી } yet, nevertheless.

ને and તથા are respectively chosen as may be more conducive to euphony and precision. As ને is the sign of the dative in circumstances where it would confound the meaning, તથા possesses more dignity and is less used in conversation.

કે is often used as a particle to connect a clause expressing the subject, matter of speech, &c. with the preceding sentence.

Ex. તેણે કહ્યું કે હા He said yes.

તોપણ is sometimes the correlate of જો the પણ of the relative being omitted when the English rendering is *though* and the correlate *yet*.

Ex. જો તે મને કેહે તોપણ હું કરૂં નહી Though he tell me, yet will I not do it.

કદાપી, &c. are used either with or without જો These are also adverbs.

તો cannot always be rendered by then.

Observe. છતાં is often used for તોપણ signifying notwithstanding.

INTERJECTION.

એ, આ, ઓ, અરે, રે, રેરે	oh! oh! oh! eh! eh! eh!	હાહા, આહાહા	ah! ah!
		હોહો	oh! oh!
		હાયહાય	alas! woe to.
		છો	a fig for!
વાહ, વાહ વાહ	very good; excellent!	હો	mind!

NUMERALS.

1	૧	એક	one	27	૨૭	શતાવીશ	twenty seven
2	૨	બે	two	28	૨૮	અઠાવીશ	twenty eight
3	૩	ત્રણ	three	29	૨૯	ઓગણત્રીશ	twenty nine
4	૪	ચાર	four	30	૩૦	ત્રીશ	thirty
5	૫	પાંચ	five	31	૩૧	એકત્રીશ	thirty one
6	૬	છ	six	32	૩૨	બત્રીશ	thirty two
7	૭	શાત	seven	33	૩૩	તેત્રીશ	thirty three
8	૮	આઠ	eight	34	૩૪	ચોત્રીશ	thirty four
9	૯	નવ	nine	35	૩૫	પાંત્રીશ	thirty five
10	૧૦	દશ	ten	36	૩૬	છત્રીશ	thirty six
11	૧૧	અગીઆર	eleven	37	૩૭	શાડત્રીશ	thirty seven
12	૧૨	બાર	twelve	38	૩૮	આડત્રીશ	thirty eight
13	૧૩	તેર	thirteen	39	૩૯	ઓગણચાલીશ	thirty nine
14	૧૪	ચઊદ	fourteen	40	૪૦	ચાલીશ	forty
15	૧૫	પંદર	fifteen	41	૪૧	એકતાલીશ	forty one
16	૧૬	શોલ	sixteen	42	૪૨	બેહેતાલીશ	forty two
17	૧૭	શતર	seventeen	43	૪૩	તેહેતાલીશ	forty three
18	૧૮	હરાડ	eighteen	44	૪૪	ચુંમાલીશ	forty four
19	૧૯	ઓગનાશ	nineteen	45	૪૫	પીશતાલીશ	forty five
20	૨૦	વીશ	twenty	46	૪૬	છેતાલીશ	forty six
21	૨૧	એકવીશ	twenty one	47	૪૭	શુડતાલીશ	forty seven
22	૨૨	બાવીશ	twenty two	48	૪૮	ઊડતાલીશ	forty eight
23	૨૩	ત્રેવીશ	twenty three	49	૪૯	ઓગણપચાશ	forty nine
24	૨૪	ચોવીશ	twenty four	50	૫૦	પચાશ	fifty
25	૨૫	પચીશ	twenty five	51	૫૧	એકાવન	fifty one
26	૨૬	છવીશ	twenty six	52	૫૨	બાવન	fifty two

53	૫૩	ત્રેપન	fifty three
54	૫૪	ચોપન	fifty four
55	૫૫	પંચાવન	fifty five
56	૫૬	છપન	fifty six
57	૫૭	શતાવન	fifty seven
58	૫૮	અઠાવન	fifty eight
59	૫૯	ઓગણુશાઠ	fifty nine
60	૬૦	શાઠ	sixty
61	૬૧	એકશઠ	sixty one
62	૬૨	બાશઠ	sixty two
63	૬૩	ત્રેશઠ	sixty three
64	૬૪	ચોશઠ	sixty four
65	૬૫	પાંશઠ	sixty five
66	૬૬	છાશઠ	sixty six
67	૬૭	શડશઠ	sixty seven
68	૬૮	અડશઠ	sixty eight
69	૬૯	અગણોતેર	sixty nine
70	૭૦	શીતેર	seventy
71	૭૧	એકોતેર	seventy one
72	૭૨	બોહોતેર	seventy two
73	૭૩	તોહોતેર	seventy three
74	૭૪	ચુંમોતેર	seventy four
75	૭૫	પંચોતેર	seventy five
76	૭૬	છોતેર	seventy six
77	૭૭	શીતોતેર	seventy seven
78	૭૮	ઈઠયોતેર	seventy eight
79	૭૯	ઓગણાશી	seventy nine
80	૮૦	હેંશી	eighty
81	૮૧	એકાશી	eighty one
82	૮૨	બાશી	eighty two
83	૮૩	ત્રાશી	eighty three
84	૮૪	ચોરાશી	eighty four
85	૮૫	પંચાશી	eighty five
86	૮૬	છાશી	eighty six
87	૮૭	શતાશી	eighty seven
88	૮૮	અઠાશી	eighty eight
89	૮૯	નેવાશી	eighty nine
90	૯૦	નેવું	ninety
91	૯૧	એકાંણું	ninety one
92	૯૨	બાંણું	ninety two
93	૯૩	ત્રાંણું	ninety three
94	૯૪	ચોરાંણું	ninety four
95	૯૫	પંચાંણું	ninety five
96	૯૬	છાંણું	ninety six
97	૯૭	શતાંણું	ninety seven
98	૯૮	અઠાંણું	ninety eight
99	૯૯	નવાંણું	ninety nine
100	૧૦૦	શો	one hundred
200	૨૦૦	બશે	two hundred
300	૩૦૦	ત્રણશે	three hundred
400	૪૦૦	ચારશે	four hundred
500	૫૦૦	પાંચશે	five hundred

600	૬૦૦	છશે	six hundred
700	૭૦૦	શાતશે	seven hundred
800	૮૦૦	આઠશે	eight hundred
900	૯૦૦	નવશે	nine hundred
1000	૧૦૦૦	હજાર	one thousand
100,000	૧૦૦૦૦૦	લાખ	one hundred thousand
10,000,000	૧૦૦૦૦૦૦૦	કરોડ	ten millions

The ordinals are formed from the above by suffixing મા. *The following are exceptions:*

પેહેલા	first
બીજો	second
ત્રીજો	third
ચોથો	fourth
છઠો	sixth

Fractions and Coins.

૧	પઈ	one pie
૧	પૈશા	one pice
-	આનો	one anna
=	બે આના	two annas
≡	ત્રણ આંના	three annas
૦।	પાવલું એટલે ચાર આંના	quarter of rupee ¼
૦।।	અડધો એટલે બે પાવલાં	half of rupee ½
૦।।।	પોણો એટલે ત્રણ પાવલાં	three quarters of rupee ¾
૧	એક રૂપૈઓ	one rupee
૧।	શાવા રૂપૈઓ	one rupee and a quarter 1¼
૧।।	ડોહોડ રૂપૈઓ	one rupee and a half 1½
૧।।।	પોણાબે રૂપૈઆ	one rupee and three quarters 1¾

Days of the Week.

રવીવાર આદીતવાર	Sunday
શોમવાર	Monday
મંગલવાર	Tuesday
બુધવાર	Wednesday
બેશપતવાર ગુરૂવાર	Thursday
શુકરવાર	Friday
શનીવાર	Saturday

Lunar Months.

ચૈત્ર	April
વઇશાખ	May
જેઠ	June
આશાડ	July
શાવણ	August
બાદરવો	September
અસ્વર	October
કારતક	November
માગશર	December
પોશ	January
માઘ	February
ફાગણ	March

Observe. The months do not correspond strictly to the English months. Dates do not therefore tally with one another. Each lunar month consists of thirty days. These are divided into portions—according to the waning and waxing of the moon. The former part is called શુદ and the latter વદ. Hence did the dates exactly correspond, which they do not, the 16th day of our month would be પડવો વદ. The following are the names of the lunar days; which are fifteen. Read after each શુદ or વદ according to the portion of the month.

1st	inst.	પડવો	9th	inst.	નોમ
2nd	,,	બીજ	10th	,,	દશેમ
3rd	,,	ત્રીજ	11th	,,	અગીઆરશ
4th	,,	ચોથ	12th	,,	બારશ
5th	,,	પાંચેમ	13th	,,	તેરશ
6th	,,	છઠ	14th	,,	ચઊદશ
7th	,,	શાતેમ	15th	,,	પુનેમ
8th	,,	આઠેમ	પુનેમ of વદ is called અમાશ.		

ETYMOLOGY.

2ND. PART.

Analysis of Words.

Gujaráti words are susceptible of analysis to a great extent, and when resolved into their constituents will in most cases be found to consist of only two consonants, sometimes of one. Compound nouns may be classified as follows :

1. Symbols of distinct individual objects are combined, e. g.

મા mother	*Combined with.*	બાપ	father	*Make the compound.*	માબાપ	parents.
દુધ milk		ભાત	rice		દુધભાત	milk and rice, (culinary).
પાન leaf		સોપારી	betal nut		પાનસોપારી	pánsopárí.
ભાઈ brother		બેહેન	sister		ભાઈબેહેન	brother and sister.
હગ purging		ઓક	sickness		હગોક	cholera.

2. Objects bearing to each other the relation expressed by the genitive or ablative cases, are represented by one compound word: e. g. ઘર house ધણી master, make the compound ઘરધણી master of the house.

3. Words significative of place are suffixed so as to form a compound word : e. g. રાજ kingdom સ્થાન place, make રાજસ્થાન capital of the kingdom.

4. Words of nearly identical signification are conjoined to increase comprehensiveness of meaning : e. g. લાગ what belongs and ભાગ share, make લાગભાગ part or lot. માલ good (household) મીલકત property (stable) make માલમીલકત property of all kinds.

5. Roots are reiterated to express greater precision or intensity : e. g. કલકલ noise of boiling, બડબડ mutter.

6. Words have suffixes nearly similar to themselves of no sig-

nification, but used merely in order to produce a chiming sound: e. g. પાંણી માણી water શાંમન ખાંમન furniture.

7. Adjectives are prefixed to substantives, so as to form a compound word: e. g. પરમ first, and ઈશ્વર God, make પરમેશ્વર Supreme God.

8. Two distinct verbal roots are conjoined: e. g. આવ come, and જા go, make આવજા coming and going, which is used as a substantive.

9. Words of the same signification are conjoined by the use of ના or ને, and express intensity: e. g. એકનો એક one only, પાપનાં પાપ very sin.

The following Table illustrates derivation for Gender.

Mas.	*Fem.*	*Neut.*	*Examples.*	
ઓ	ઈ	ઉં	કુતરો રી રૂં	dog.
final. cons.			બ્રામણ બ્રામણી	brámaṇ.
			મુશલમાન મુશલમાની	músalmán.
ઈ	એણ		કુણબી કુણબેણ	kúṇbí
final. cons.			લવાણો લવાણેણ	laváṇo (caste).
ઓ			વાઘ વાઘેણ	tiger.
ઈઓ			કાછીઓ કાછીએણ	káchío (caste).
final. cons.	ણી		ઊંટ ઊંટણી	camel.
			ભુંડ ભુંડણી	pig.
ઈ	આણી		ધણી ધણીઆણી	master.
final. cons.			ઠાકોર ઠાકરાણી	a chief.
			પટેલ પટલાણી	patél.
			રજપુત રજપુતાણી	rajpút (caste.)

It will be observed that the *specific* formations are made according to euphony; also that in forming the feminine, the long vowel is adopted.

Substantives derived from Substantives and Verbs by Suffixes.

1. Objects.

(Comprehending occupation, office, circumstance, place, &c.)

Suffix.	*Origin.*	*Signif.*	*Comp.*	*Signification.*
ઈ	પટેલ	patél.	પટેલી	patélship.
	ગુલામ	slave.	ગુલામી	slavery.
	દસ્તુર	custom.	દસ્તુરી	customary fee.
ણુ	જમ	eat.	જમણુ	meal, feast.
વટ	ભોગ	enjoy.	ભોગવટ	right of enjoyment.
આણુ	ઊઘર	collect.	ઊઘરાણુ	collection.
આલ	ઘડી	ghăḍí.	ઘડીઆલ	instrument for computing the ghăḍí (watch).
વો	છોડ	shrub.	છોડવો	small shrub.
ક	બેઠ	sit.	બેઠક	seat.
ઓ	રોપ	plant.	રોપો	a plant.
ડો	ગામ	village.	ગામડો	hamlet.
કાર	આવ	come.	આવકાર	kind reception.
ઓ	ફેર	turn.	ફેરો	turning.
ણું	ધાવણું	suck.	ધાવણું	suckling.
ઘાટ	માલે	Málé.	માલેઘાટ	Málégháṭ.
સ્થાન	રાજ	kingdom.	રાજસ્થાન	capital.
ઘડ	પાવો	Pávo.	પાવોઘડ	Pavoghaḍ.
પુર	શોલા	Solá.	શોલાપુર	Solápúr.
ખાણું	કેદ	confine.	કેદખાણું	prison.
આંત	વરશ	year.	વરશાંત	yearly stipend.

2. Subjects.

(Comprehending all that sustain office, trade, occupations, &c.)

Suffix.	*Origin.*	*Signif.*	*Comp.*	*Signification.*
ઈ	કારભાર	office.	કારભારી	officer.
	સુરત	Surat.	સુરતી	Surat man.
	ઘડીઆલ	watch.	ઘડીઆલી	watch maker.
વાળો	દુધ	milk.	દુધવાળો	milk man.
	ટોપી	cap, &c.	ટોપીવાળો	wearer of a cap.
વાન	ગાડી	gáḍi.	ગાડીવાન	driver of a gáḍi.
યો	રશોઈ	cooked food.	રશોઈયો	cook.
કર	વણ	weave.	વણકર	weaver.
નાર	લખ	write.	લખનાર	writer.
ઈઓ	બડબડ	prate.	બડબડીયો	prater.
	ખેપ	trip.	ખેપીઓ	a messenger, express.
ઊત	ખેડ	till.	ખેડુત	tiller.
આરો	ચીત	draw.	ચીતારો	draughtsman.
	રંગ	paint.	રંગારો	painter.
ગાર	મદદ	assistance.	મદદગાર	assistant.
ગર	કારી	work.	કારીગર	workman.
દાર	દફતર	record.	દફતરદાર	a keeper of records.
બંદ	હથીઆર	weapon.	હથીઆરબંધ	one wearing weapons.
બી	ધો	wash.	ધોબી	washerman.
વો	બંધ	shut.	બંધવો	a prisoner, slave.
ડો *	વેરાગી	Vérágí.	વેરાગડો	Vérágí (contemptuous).

* ડો is a real diminutive, and is applied to individuals in way of contempt.

Substantives derived from Verbs and Adjectives.

3. Abstractness.

(Comprehending condition, quality, &c.)

Suffix.	*Origin.*	*Signif.*	*Compound.*	*Signification.*
તા	શુધ	pure.	શુધતા	purity.
ણ	ઊંડા	deep.	ઊંડાણ	depth.
ક	થંડ	cold.	થંડક	coldness.
શ	મીઠા	sweet.	મીઠાશ	sweetness.
આઈ	ખાટ	sour.	ખટાઈ	sourness.
આત	કઠણ	hard.	કઠણાત	hardness.
ઈ	ગરમ	hot.	ગરમી	heat.
તી	ગણ	reckon.	ગણતી	reckoning.
પો	અંધો	blind.	અંધાપો	blindness.
તર	ભણ	study.	ભણતર	study.
પણ	ડાયા	wise.	ડાયાપણ	wisdom.
પણ	ઘડ	old.	ઘડપણ	old age.
રણ	જાગ	watch.	જાગરણ	watchfulness.
ણ	ચલ	move.	ચલણ	motion, currency.
ણી	સીવ	sow.	સીવણી	sowing.
ત	રમ	play.	રમત	play.
આટ	કલકલ	a noise.	કલકલાટ	a noise.
ખડ	ભાંજ	break.	ભાંજખડ	final settlement of a dispute.
મણ	શીખા	instruct.	શીખામણ	instruction.

Adjectives derived from Substantives, Verbs, and Prepositions,

Pre.	*Orig.*	*Signification.*	*Comp.*	*Signification.*
યો	ભુખ	hunger.	ભુખ્યો	hungry.
નો	માંહે	within.	માંહેનો	interior.
ઈ	ધરમ	religion.	ધરમી	religious.
ડો	દેખાવ	show.	દેખાવડો	showy.
ડો	મેલાવ	make to meet.	મેલાવડો	
ણો	ચીક	gluten.	ચીકણો	glutinous.
આલો	દુધ	milk.	દુધાલો	milky.
આળ	લોહી	blood.	લોહીઆળ	that has blood.
ઈએલ	અડ	obstacle.	અડીએલ	obstinate.
ળ	ખરચા	expense.	ખરચાળ	extravagant.
ખોર	લડાઈ	quarrel.	લડાઈખોર	quarrelsome.
વડો	આ	this.	આવડો	such a one.
કણો	માર	beat.	મારકણો	addicted to beating.
લુ	દઆ	pity.	દઆલુ	pitiful.
ઓ	આગલ	before.	આગલો	preceding.
ઈલો	રશ	juice.	રશીલો	juicy.
ગણો*	ચાર	four.	ચારગણો	fourfold.
માન'	બુધી	wisdom.	બુધીમાન	wise.
વાન	ભાએગ	fortune.	ભાએગવાન	fortunate.
મણો	લજા	shame.	લજામણો	shameful.
કારી'	સુખ	pleasure.	શુખકારી	producing pleasure.
દાએક'	દુખ	pain.	દુખદાએક	painful.
ક	ઊપદેશ	instruction.	ઊપદેશક	instructor.
જોગ'	વીશ્વાશ	faith.	વીશ્વાશજોગ	faithful, worthy of faith.
ઈતો	ઓલખ	know.	ઓલખીનો	one acquainted.
મંત	બુધી	wisdom.	બુધીમંત	wise.

Pre.	Orig.	Signification.	Comp.	Signigcation.
વંત	દયા	mercy.	દયાવંત	merciful.
મંદ	દોલત	riches.	દોલતમંદ	rich.
આતુર	શોક	grief.	શોકાતુર	full of grief.
આરો	દુખી	afflicted.	દુખીઆરો	an afflicted person.
રૂત	જાગ	watch.	જાગરૂત	watchful.

Derivatives formed by Prefixes from Adjectives or Substantives.

	Pre.	Orig.	Signif.	Comp.	Signification.
Negatives or privatives.	અ	જાણ્યો	knowing.	અજાણ્યો	ignorant, unknown.
	અણ	શમજ્યો	of understanding.	અણશમજ્યો	without understanding.
	અપ	માન	honour.	અપમાન	disgrace.
	નીર	ઉપાય	remedy.	નીરઉપાય	remediless.
	બે	ફીકર	care.	બેફીકર	careless.
	ગેર	વાજબી	just.	ગેરવાજબી	unjust.
	ના	ઉમેદ	hope.	નાઉમેદ	hopeless.
Modifications of quality.	બદ	ચાલ	conduct.	બદચાલ	bad conduct.
	સુ	મારગ	road.	સુમારગ	good road.
	સ	ચાલ	conduct.	સચાલ	(metaphorically) bad conduct.
	કુ	વશન	habit.	કુવશન	evil habit.
	ક	ચાલ	conduct.	કચાલ	evil conduct.
	દુર	આચરણ	conduct, &c.	દુરાચરણ	depraved conduct, &c.
	અવ	ગુણ	quality.	અવગુણ	mischief, evil quality.
Own and foreign.	સ્વ	દેશ	country.	સ્વદેશ	own country.
	પર	„	„	પરદેશ	foreign country.

Observe. 1. According to the analogy of language, affixes should only be made specifically, i. e. Sanscrit affixes to Sanscrit words, &c.

2. ઓ is always changed into આ before making a suffix.

3. The above derivations are made on the principle of utility to the student more than on the principles of philosophy.

4. The numerous suffixes drawn from the Sanscrit, the Hindustani, as well as those peculiar to the language, afford the writer fruitful means of invention.

Derivation of words.

1. Simple.

Rule 1. When the root of the verb has a consonant both for its ultimate and penultimate (these being mostly neuter), derivation is made according to the following rules:

1 The active is formed from the neuter by inserting the vowel આ between the ultimate and penultimate consonants.

2 The passive is formed from the neuter by suffixing આ. The Causative is formed from the Passive by suffixing વ or ડ; and the double Causative is formed from the Causative, by eliding the penultimate and suffixing વ or ડ as may be more euphonous.

These rules are illustrated as follows:

Neuter.		*Active.*	*Passive.*	*Causative.*
melt.	ગલ	ગાલ	ગલા	ગલાવ
digest.	પચ	પાચ	પચા	પચાવ
fall.	પડ	પાડ	પડા	પડાવ
burn.	બલ	બાલ	બલા	બલાવ
heat.	તપ	તાપ	તપા	તપાવ
swim.	તર	તાર	તરા	તરાવ

Neuter.		*Active.*	*Passive.*	*Causative.*
dash against.	અફળ	અફાળ	અફળા	અફળાવ
boil.	ઊકળ	ઊકાળ	ઊકળા	ઊકળાવ
descend.	ઊતર	ઊતાર	ઊતરા	ઊતરાવ
improve.	સુધર	સુધાર	સુધરા	સુધરાવ
press.	દબ	દાબ	દબા	દબાવ
bend.	વળ	વાળ	વળા	વળાવ

Observe. I. The rendering of several English Verbs is the same for active and neuter, as heat, bend, boil, &c. but sometimes a different verb or a periphrasis is needed; e. g. the rendering of ઊતાર is, cause to descend, or to lower.

2. There are a few active verbs of a neuter form, as લખ write. From these of course no active form can be derived.

3. The double causatives are seldom needed and therefore not inserted. The following are specimens બળવાવ, ગળવાવ.

RULE. 2. When the penultimate is any vowel save આ (such verbs being generally active) no active can of course be formed therefrom, but the Passives and Causatives are derived in the above way.

Active.		*Passive.*	*Causative.*
draw.	ખેંચ	ખેંચા	ખેંચાવ
toast, &c.	શેક	શેકા	શેકાવ
sow.	સીવ	સીવા	સીવાડ

RULE. 3. If the penultimate be આ it is dropped in the formation of the passive, and અ is substituted for it. If the આ be initial then the full અ is expressed. If it be not initial but following a consonant, then the substitute is considered as inherent in the consonant of the derivative and is therefore not expressed.

Active.		*Passive.*	*Causative.*
draw.	આણ	અણા	અણાવ
drive.	હાંક	હંકા	હંકાવ
cook.	રાંધ	રંધા	રંધાવ
know.	જાણ	જણા	જણાવ
draw.	તાણ	તણા	તણાવ
sow.	વાવ	વવા	વવાડ

RULE. 4. If the ultimate of the root be આ (such verbs being mostly active) the Passive is formed by eliding the vowel, and suffixing વા. The Causative is formed in the usual way.

Active.		*Passive.*	*Causative.*
sing.	ગા	ગવા	ગવાડ
be.	થા	થવા	થવાડ
rush.	ધા	ધવા	ધવાડ
eat.	ખા	ખવા	ખવાડ
go.	જા	જવા	જવાડ

RULE. 5. If the ultimate letter be a vowel not આ, it is allowed to continue, and the Passive is formed by the suffix of વા.

Active.		*Passive.*	*Causative.*
say.	કેહે	કેહેવા	કેહેવાડ
flow.	વેહે	વેહેવા	વેહેવાડ
suffer.	શેહે	શેહેવા	શેહેવાડ
fear.	ખીહી	ખીહીવા	ખીહીવાડ
rot.	કોહો	કોહોવા	કોહોવાડ
sleep.	શુ	શુવા	શુવાડ
see.	જો	જોવા	જોવાડ
wash.	ધો	ધોવા	ધોવાડ

Exceptions of Derivation.

There are a few neuter verbs which form their Active and Causative by inserting એ instead of આ; e. g. from ઊછર neuter, is derived ઊછેર active, bring up; from ઘસડ neuter, is derived ઘસેડ drag, &c.

Table illustrative of verbal derivations.

	Orig.	*Act.*	*Pas.*	*Caus.*	*Caus.*
1. ult. and pen. cons.	વલ	વાલ	વલા	વલાવ	વલવાડ
2. pen. vowel not આ.	ખેંચ		ખેંચા	ખેંચાવ	ખેંચવાવ
3. penult. vowel આ.	આણ		અણા	અણાવ	અણવાવ
	હાંક		હંકા	હંકાવ	હંકવાવ
4. ultimate આ.	ગા		ગવા	ગવાડ	ગવડાવ
5. ultimate vowel not આ.	કેહે		કેહેવા	કેહેવાડ	કેહેવડાવ
	ખીહી		ખીહીવા	ખીહીવાડ	ખીહીવડાવ
	શુ		શુવા	શુવાડ	શુવડાવ
Exception.	ઊછર	ઊછેર	ઊછેરા	ઊછેરાવ	ઊછેરવાડ

2. *Compound Verbs.*

Verbs of this language are susceptible of compounding to an indefinite extent. The principle of compounding is uniform viz.

The past compound participle in its abbreviated form, of the verb to be modified, is prefixed to the verb which modifies. It is then in its compound state conjugated as one verb. The compounded verb may itself also be compounded by another verb.

The compound verb expresses modification either of time or action. It is also used to express complexity of action, such as is expressed in English by two individual verbs or by adverbs.

The susceptibility of composition of the verb furnishes fruitful means for the future improvement of the language. The more important compounds in general use are as follows:

To remain. રેહેવું } ચુકવું } in composition signify finished action.

Ex. 1. હું માહારો કાગલ લખી રહીશ I shall have written my letter.

2. હું માહારૂં ઘર બાંધી ચુકો I have finished building my house.

To place. મુકવું 1. Retains its literal signification. 2. Metaphorically signifies settledness, decision, with the involved idea that the action will not be resumed.

Ex. 1. હું રાખી મુકીશ I will lay it by (reserve).

2. મે કહી મુકું I have said *once for all.*

To cast, to throw down. નાંખવું or લાખવું } 1. Retains its literal meaning. 2. Expresses metaphorically, summary or downright action.

Ex. 1. મારી નાંખવું to beat down, (kill).

2. જે કેહેવાનું હતું તે મે કહી નાંખ્યું I have said (summarily and *downright)* what I had to say.

To see જોવું, signifies investigation.

Ex. ચાખી જુઓ Taste and see.

To sit. બેશવું 1. Retains its literal meaning. 2. Metaphorically, the fact of settling down in action.

Ex. 1. તે કીચડમાં ડુબી બેઠો He sunk down in the mud.

2. તે આશા રાખી બેઠો He has settled down in the hope.

To go. જવું. 1. Retains its literal meaning.
2. Expresses dispatch in the performance of the action.

Ex. 1. તે એમ કહી ગયો He said thus and went.

2. તે શમજી જશે He will quickly understand.

To take લેવું, signifies prompt and precise execution of action, such as is expressed by the adverbs up, down, or by the phrase "take and &c."

Ex. 1. ખાઈલ્યો Eat up. 2. લખીલ્યો Write down.

2. આ કાપડ કાપીલ્યો Take and cut this cloth.

To give દેવું, expresses metaphorically, a certain freedom or readiness of action analogous to the act of giving.

Ex. 1. મેં કહી દીધું I spoke out (i. e. revealed).

2. તે મુકી દો Leave that alone.

Add to the above ઊઠવું, આવવું, કાહાડવું, &c. the modifications produced by which are deducible from their signification. In fact, composition may be made to any extent, each word retaining its literal meaning. The above are chiefly metaphorical.

III. SYNTAX.

1st. Part.

Substantive.

1. A Substantive signifying weight, measure, &c. precedes the substantive to which it relates, and is placed in the nominative or accusative case.

Ex. 1. બે શેર અનાજ Two seers of corn.

2. ચાર ગજ બનાત Four guj of broad cloth.

3. ત્રણ વીઘાં જમીન Three acres of land.

2. When of two (or more) Substantives, one is a proper name, and the other a common name expressing a proper attribute, as of title, office, &c. the proper name is placed first.

Ex. 1. વીક્ટોરીઆ રાણી Queen Victoria.

2. ગોવીંદ વકીલ Govind Vakil.

3. A Substantive not proper, having other substantives or other parts of speech *placed in apposition and qualifying it*, is placed after them in its appropriate case, while the qualificatory words precede it and are placed in the nominative.

Ex. સુરતનો રેહેવાશી શરકારનો કારભારી એક બરામણને હું ઓલખું છઊ I know a Bráman, a native of Surat, a Government Officer.

Note 1. Words in apposition generally but not uniformly assume the following relative position :

1. Place, 2 circumstance, 3 office, 4 character, 5 caste, lastly name.

NOTE 2. If the qualifying substantives, &c. in apposition are very numerous so as to render obscure their connection with the substantive they qualify, the definitive pronoun એવો, with or without a numeral, is employed as a bond of connection.

4. The Substantive immediately follows the adjective or adjectival part of speech, by which it is qualified.

Ex. શારો છોકરો A good boy.

Excep. In mercantile correspondence Substantives signifying coin, &c. are placed before numerals.

Ex. રૂપીઆ બે Two rupees.

5. When the Substantive is the subject of which the adjective or adjectival part of speech is predicated, it *precedes* such part of speech.

Ex. આ છોકરો શારોછે This boy is good.

NOTE. This rule as well as the preceding has its counterpart in English.

6. A Substantive of the first declension (see Substantive) representing several objects, when qualified by an adjective or an adjectival part of speech in the plural number, or by a numeral, is placed in the singular or plural number ad libitum.

Ex. ચાર માણસ Four men. 2. શારાં માણસો Good men.

NOTE. For the sake of precision and the preservation of the analogy of language, the invariable use of the plural form to represent several objects, is greatly desirable and accords with the practice of the most accurate speakers. It sometimes happens that a substantive in a plural form may be mistaken for another substantive with a singular termination; e. g. the plural of હાથ is હાથો; this word signifies a handle, and in such a case of ambiguity the plural form is not to be preserved.

7. The Substantive precedes the preposition which governs it, and is placed in the case appropriate to its government. (see preposition).

Ex. 1. ઘોડાપર On the horse.

2. છોકરાનીપાશે To or near the boy.

8. When several Substantives mutually connected, understood collectively, are equally governed by a single preposition, the last substantive alone is put in the case appropriate to its government, the others retaining their nominative form.

Ex. જુઠો, ઠગારો, ચોર તથા લુચ્ચાની શાથે વાત કરવી નહી We should not converse with a liar, a cheat, a thief, or a blackguard.

Note. When a definitive pronoun (see note 2. Rule 3.) with or without a numeral is used to sustain the burthen of substantives used collectively, it alone is placed in the case appropriate to its government, all the substantives being in the nominative case. As, in the above example read લુચ્ચો એયોની શાથે.

9. If of two Substantives, the one be the subject of the verb, and the other the predicate, that which is the subject is put first.

Ex. શબ્દ ઈશ્વર હતો The word was God.

10. The Substantive either mediately or immediately *precedes* the verb, whether it be its subject or object. If it be its subject, it is placed in the nominative case; and if it be its object, in either the accusative or dative case, according to the government of the verb (see verb).

Ex. 1. છોકરો શીખેછે The boy learns.

2. મેતાજી છોકરાને શીખવેછે The métáji teaches the boy.

Note. As the Dative case is formed by the proposition ને, Rule 8 and note are here applicable.

11. The subject of the verb (either direct or medial), is generally placed at the head of a sentence.

Ex. રાજા પ્રધાનને મોકલશે The king will send the minister.

NOTE. Words qualificatory of the verb, as of time, mode, &c. often precede the substantive which is the subject.

Ex. ઘણા દાહાડાપછી રાજા &c. After several days the king &c.

12. If of two Substantives the one be the immediate object of the verb in the accusative case, and the other be the final object in the dative case, that which is the final object is generally placed *first*.

Ex. ચાકરને કાગલ આપો Give the letter to the servant.

13. If of two Substantives the one be the immediate object of the verb and the other be the final object, both being in the Dative case, that which is the immediate object, is placed *first*.

Ex. તેણે પોતાના મીત્રને હાકમને શોંપી આપ્યો He delivered up his friend to the Judge.

14. The Substantive significative of time is sometimes used in the nominative instead of the ablative.

Ex. હુ આખો દાહાડો ત્યાં રહ્યો I stopped there all day.

ADJECTIVE.

1. The Adjective agrees with the substantive or word used substantively, in gender, number, and case, as far as it is susceptible of modification.

Ex. 1. ડાહ્યા પુરૂશનું Of a wise man

2. શારાં છોકરાં Good children.

Excep. 1. The Adjective is used in the plural masculine with a masculine substantive to express respect.

Ex. માહારા બાપ શારા છે My father is well. Also with a few substantives of plurality; e. g. શારા ગઊં Good wheat.

2. The Adjective is used in the plural neuter with a feminine substantive to express respect.

Ex. માહારી મા શારાં છે My mother is well.

3. An Adjective qualifying two or more substantives, of either the same or different genders, agrees only in gender and number with the substantive which it immediately precedes.

Ex. જો હીયાં ડાયો પુરશ કે સ્રી હોઅ્ય તો કોહો If there be a wise man or woman here, say so.

Note. This license of language, whereby an adjective is used once to qualify more than one substantive, is more restrained in this language than in English.

4. An Adjective predicated of several substantives, or substantival parts of speech, of the same gender, *used collectively*, is placed in the plural number and in the same gender. If they be of different genders, then it is placed in the neuter gender plural.

Ex. 1. માહારો બાઈ તથા માહારો દીકરો શારા છે My brother and my son are well.

2. માહારો બાઈ તથા માહારી બેહેન શારાં છે My brother and my sister are well.

5. An Adjective predicated of several substantives, or substantival parts of speech used disjunctively, agrees with the last expressed word.

Ex. જો ગાઅ્યે કે ઘોડો લંગડો હોઅ્યે If the cow or horse be lame.

6. An Adjective predicated of a plural pronoun or numeral involving different genders, is placed in the plural number and neuter gender.

Ex. હમે શારાં છુઈઅ્યેં We (male and female) are well.

7. An Adjective used adverbially to qualify an adjective or verb, agrees with the substantive in gender, number and case.

Ex. ઘણી શારી છોકરી A very good girl.

8. An Adjective predicated of the infinitive mood of whatever number or gender, is placed in the singular number and neuter gender.

Ex. તમારે કંઇએક ધંધો કરવો શારૂં છે It is good for you to do some work.

NOTE. In sentences of the above nature, the adjective is sometimes really predicated of the substantive and not of the infinitive, in which case it of course agrees with the substantive.

Ex. આ ધંધો કરવો શારો છે This is a good work (occupation) to do.

9. Adjectives, significative of desire, appetency, repleteness, similarity, and of kindred ideas, govern the genitive. e. g. ભુખ્યો, તરશો, લાલચુ, &c.

10. Adjectives significative of difference, alienation, averseness, distance, and other kindred ideas, govern the ablative; e. g. જુદો, વેગળો, નીરાળુ.

11. Adjectives following substantives, to which they bear any of the various relations of the genitive (see Substantive) govern the genitive.

Ex 1. ઘણા દાહાડાનો ભુખ્યો Hungry of many days (for).

2. પઈશાનો અભીમાની Proud of (on account of) money.

3. તાવનો માંદો Sick of fever (origin).

4. માણુશનો બનાવેલો દેવ A god made of (by) man.

---

3. PRONOUN.

1. Pronouns when used as substantives, are subject to the same rules as substantives relatively to other parts of speech. See Substantive.

2. Pronouns used as adjectives are subject to the same rules as adjectives relatively to other parts of speech. See Adjective.

3. An adjectival pronoun qualifying a substantive which is already qualified by an adjective, precedes the adjective.

Ex. માહારાં બધાં ઘરો All my houses.

4. A definitive pronoun when representing a whole sentence or an undefined object, is placed in the singular number and neuter gender if so declinable, and if not susceptible of such declination it is nevertheless to be considered as in such number and gender. See Adjective note of rule 8.

5. The personal pronoun precedes the substantive with which it is in apposition in the nominative case irrespectively of the case in which the substantive may be placed.

Ex. હું ગરીબ માણસપર દયા કર Pity me, a poor man.

Note 1. In order to obviate the obscurity which would frequently ensue from the use of the personal pronouns in apposition with the substantives, the following two media are adopted. 1. The pronoun is placed in the nominative case in apposition with the substantive likewise in the nominative, and again repeated after it in the case in which it may be governed. 2. The sentence may be broken into two by the use of the substantive verb.

Ex. 1. હું ગરીબ માંણુશ માહારાપર દયા કર Have pity on me, a poor man.

2. હું ગરીબ માંણુશ છુઉં &c. I am a poor man, &c.

Note. 2. Where there is a disjunctive sense between the pronoun and the substantive, the participle છતાં or થઈને used as a disjunctive conjunction follows the substantive.

Ex. તમે બરામણ થઈને નથી શમજતા? Do not you, a Bráman, understand?

6. The personal pronouns are generally expressed before the verb in composition, as being essential to perspicuity.

7. When two or more verbs occur in the same tenses or in tenses having the same individual subject, the pronoun is expressed before the first verb, but is not required before the subsequent verbs.

Note 1. This rule holds good although one of the verbs may demand a nominative as its subject, and the other demand an ablative case as its medial subject. Ex. તે કાલે આવ્યો ને કેહું કે &c.

Note 2. Observe; if in violation of this rule the pronoun be repeated, it is impossible to preclude a mental reference to another person than the subject of the first verb. The last person *may* be different from the first, if the sentence be as follows, Ex. તે કાલે આવ્યો ને તેણે કહું.

8. The third personal pronoun relative to a substantive is used respectively of the substantive which it represents, and is therefore in all cases placed subsequent to it.

Remark. Hence if the respective construction of sentences in the Gujaráti and English languages demand it, the substantive must be placed in the former where the pronoun is placed in the latter, and vice versá.

Ex. 1. જો કોઈ માણસ જ્ઞાન શોધે તો તેને મળે May be rendered in English by a converse sentence; as, a man will find wisdom, if he seek for it.

2. માણસ પાહાડ ઊપર ચડે તે કરતાં તેને ઊતરવું સેહેલું છે. A man can descend a hill easier than he can climb it.

Observe. If the above rule be violated, the reference of the pronoun to some other person than that represented, is unavoidable.

9. The relative pronoun જે is placed before the substantive or pronoun to which it anticipatively relates, and is in that position subject to no government.

10 The relative pronoun જે is placed after a substantive, to which it reflectively relates, and is then subject to government.

11. The relative pronouns are not expressed when their expression is unessential to perspicuity, their use being rendered superfluous by the use of their correlates.

12. The correlates and relatives have each their appropriate government, &c.

Preposition.

1. The preposition follows the substantive or other parts of speech which it governs.

2. The declinable preposition નો follows the word which signifies the subject of possession, and agrees in gender, number, and case, with the word which expresses the object of possession.

Ex. 1. રાજાની વાડી Garden of the king.

2. ઝાડનાં પાતરાં Leaves of the tree.

3. The declinable preposition નો when governed by a preposition, is placed in the form appropriate to its government viz. ના or ની (see preposition).

4. A preposition when governing several substantives or substantival parts of speech, is not employed before each of them but only before the last expressed.

Ex. ચીન હીંદુશથાન તથા વીલાતમાં હું ફરી ફરીને આવ્યો I have returned from travels in China, Hindustan, and Europe.

Excep. If it be intended to specify each individually, and not to predicate of them collectively, the use of the preposition with each substantive is allowable.

Ex. સુરતમાં તથા મુંબાઈમાં માહારાં સગાં ઘણાં છે I have many relatives in Surat and Bombay.

5. The preposition નેા is frequently used both in the singular and plural, without a substantive, the substantive expressive of thing or person being understood.

Ex. શેહેર માંનાંને હું એાળખતેા નથી I do not know those of the city.

Adverbs.

1. Adverbs qualifying adjectives immediately precede them.

2. Adverbs expressive of mode of action precede the verb they qualify, either immediately or by medium of the subject or object of the verb as may be most conducive to perspicuity.

Note. This rule comprehends all forms of expression used adverbially.

3. Interrogative adverbs generally precede the verb without any medium.

4. Relative adverbs of time, place, and comparison, as also their correlates, are placed at the head of their respective sentences.

5. Where the correlate adverb is expressed, the relative adverb is not expressed, save where its use is essential to perspicuity.

6. If two relative adverbs be expressed, the two correlates are likewise expressed.

4. Verb.

1. The verb having a nominative as its subject, agrees with the nominative in all its simple tenses in number and person, and in all its participial tenses, in number, person, and gender.

Ex. 1. મેતા લખેછે The clerk is writing.

2. પાંતરાં ખડતાં હતાં The leaves were falling.

Excep. 1. See adjective rule 1.

Note. Where the nominative is not expressed, but the idea is comprehended of work, thing, &c. or when the verb is used impersonally, it is put in the neuter gender.

Ex. મને પેટમાં દુખતું હતું I had a pain in my stomach.

2. If the verb be transitive having no nominative but an ablative as a medial subject, it is placed in the third person if the tense be compound, and agrees with the word which is its immediate object in gender and number.

Ex. મે છોકરાને માર્યોછે I have beaten the boy.

Note. 1. The infinitive mood of an active verb having a medial subject expressed or understood and governing an object, is comprehended under this rule.

Ex. છોકરાંએ પોતાનાં માબાપને માંનવાં Children should obey their parents.

Note 2. Transitive verbs of various significations are also used to denote simple action without reference to particular objects, in which case they are placed in the neuter gender.

Ex. તેણે કહું પણ મે માંન્યું નહી He said, but I did not mind, &c. Neuter verbs are used in a similar way.

3. A neuter or passive verb, having two nominatives, agrees with the nominative which is its primary subject in gender, number, and person.

Ex. તે વેશ ધરીને સ્રી માલુમ પડ્યો He, putting on a disguise, appeared to be a woman.

4. If the verb have for one of two or more nominatives, the first personal pronoun, it is placed in the first person plural, irrespectively of the persons of the other nouns.

Ex. હું ને માહારો ભાઈ જઈશું I and my brother will go.

5. If the verb have for one of two or more nominatives, the second personal pronoun, it is placed in the second person plural irrespectively, &c.

Ex. તું ને તમારી બેહેન કેવારે આવશો? When wilt thou and thy sister come?

6. The intransitive verb in its participial tenses, having a plural personal pronoun or a numeral involving different genders as its subject, or the transitive verb having the same as its object in its aorist tenses, is placed in the plural number and neuter gender.

Ex. હમે આવ્યાં છઈયે We (man and woman) have come.

7. The verb in its participial tenses, having two or more nominatives as its subjects or two more objective cases as its objects of the same or different genders according to rule 2. used in a collective sense, is subject to the same rules as the adjective (vide adjective rule 4).

Ex. 1. માહારો ભાઈ ને માહારી બેહેન હવડાં મરી ગયાંછે. My brother and sister are just dead.

2. માહારો બાપ તથા માહારો કાકો આવ્યાછે My father and my uncle have come.

8. The verb in its participial tenses, having two or more nominatives as its subjects or two or more objective cases as its objects of the same or different genders according to rule 2. used in a disjunctive sense, is subject to the same rule as the adjective.

Ex. માહારા દીકરાને કે માહારી દીકરીને તમે જોઈ? Have you seen either my son or my daughter?

9. The verb occupies the last position in the sentence, whether it be predicative, imperative, or interrogative, of which it sustains the burthen.

NOTE. Hence the participle, whether expressing action contemporaneous with or preceding the action of the verb, being incapable of sustaining the burthen of the sentence, must be placed before it. This remark is applicable to every form of expression however simple or complex.

1. *Predicative.*

Ex. સુરજ પ્રથવીને પ્રકાશ કરે છે. The sun enlightens the earth.

2. *Interrogative.*

Ex તમે વીલાત કે વારે જશો? When will you go to Europe?

3. *Imperative.*

Ex. માહારી પાશે ચોપડી લાવો Bring the book to me.

Excep. 1. In a negative sentence, the verb is generally placed before the negative particle નથી, and frequently before the other particles as well as the particle નો, also a few words used adverbially, as ખરૂં truly, &c.

Excep. 2. When there is in sense a repetition of the action of the verb, provided that the verb have been previously expressed, the latter verb is sometimes omitted. This is not elegant, and though allowable in familiar conversation, is not to be tolerated in composition. Neither is the anticipative understanding of a verb, so common in English, congenial to Gujaráti.

10. The verb when expressing transitive action or action passing over to an object, or issuing in a point, or mental states, having an external object, or impartative action of any kind governs the dative.

Ex. માહારા ચાકરને મોકલો Send my servant.

11. The verb when expressing action that does not pass over to or affect its object, governs the accusative.

Ex · મે વીચાર કીધેા I havė considered.

(See Acc. and Dat).

2ND. PART.*

Analysis of Compound Sentences.

1. When of a compound sentence one clause is dependent on a preposition, it is put before the other clause or clauses which are related to it.

NOTE I. This comprehensive rule embraces a most important class of sentences viz. those which express comparison, priority or subsequence in place or time, similitude, &c.

NOTE 2. Hence it frequently happens that the clauses of sentences of such import sustain mutually different positions, and contain mutually different elements in the English and Gujaráti languages.

Comparison.

Ex. 1. માણુશ દેાડે તે કરતાં કેટલાંએક જાાનવરેા જલદી ચાલી શકેછે Some animals can walk quicker than a man can run.

2. ગુજરાતી બેાલવા કરતાં હું વાંચી શકું છુઊં I am able to read Gujaráti better than I speak it.

Place.

Ex. માહારી વાડીમાં જાહાડ છે તેની પછવાડે એક માંણુશ સુતેા છે A man is sleeping behind the tree which is in my garden.

---

* The rules comprised under this part, which is intended to develope the syntax of sentences, are strictly deducible from the rules of the first part, and therefore their introduction may seem unnecessary. The student of a new language differing so entirely from his own, will however be grateful for deductions made for him. If left to himself, he refuses to admit his own conclusions from grammatical premises, and needs the evidence of sense to assist his own logic.

Time.

Ex. ગઈ રાતે મને હુંઘ આવ્યાપછી ચંદ્ર ગ્રહણ થયું An eclipse of the moon took place after I had gone to sleep last night.

Similitude.

Ex. જેયો ઢોંગે કરીને ધરમ કરેછે તેયોની પઠે ન કરો Do not imitate those who practise religion from ostentation.

2. When of a sentence, one clause is prefaced by a relative pronoun or adverb or any other relative part of speech, or when such part of speech is understood and the other is prefaced by its correlate, the former clause is placed first.

N. B. Hence &c. see note 2. rule 1.

NOTE. This comprehensive rule embraces an important class of sentences viz. those which express hypothesis, those which relate to persons, quality, quantity, degree, place, time, mode, similitude, &c.

Time.

Ex. તમે હુકમ આપો તાંહાં શુધી તે જશે નહી He will not go until you give the command.

Quantity.

Ex. જેટલું તમે મને આપ્યું તેટલું હું તમને પાછું આપું છુઉ I give you back as much as you have given me.

Quality.

Ex. જેવો તમારો બાપ વીધ્યાવાન હતો તેવા તમે થાઓ Be as learned as your father was.

NOTE. When the idea expressed by any relative part of speech is in the mind of the speaker subsidiary to some other idea already expressed, its expression is likewise subsequent.

Ex. I. તમે બુધીવાન થાઓ Be you wise (primary).

2. જેવો તમારો બાપ પણ બુધીવાન હતો As your father also was wise (subsidiary).

One of two theories may serve to elucidate this fact, viz. first that after the analogy of the relative pronoun, the other relative parts of speech have a reflective as well as anticipative relation, or secondly that the correlate with its appended sentence, is to be understood as following the first clause.

3. When a sentence occurs whose clauses are conjoined by the disjunctive virtual conjunctions છતાં, થયને (notwithstanding), or any word of tantamount meaning, the clause which these words serve to disjoin is placed first.

N. B. Hence, &c. see note 2. rule 1.

Ex. પરમેશ્વરે માંણુશોને ઘણો ઊપકાર કરયા છતાં પણ માણુશો તેને માંનતાં નથી

Men do not reverence God, notwithstanding that He does them much good.

Observe. તોપણ being a correlate is contained in rule 2.

4. When of a compound sentence, one clause contains the subject and the other the predicate, that which contains the subject is placed first, however complex the nature of the subject or predicate may be.

N. B. Hence, &c. see note 2. rule 1.

NOTE. Although the correlate pronoun તે and the definitive એ, એવું, are made use of to sustain the burthen of a clause and thence become themselves the subject of the predicate, it will be conducive to perspicuity to consider in each case the whole clause, together with the sustaining pronoun as the subject. Hence under this rule are comprehended clauses, which independently contain both subject and predicate, but which relatively to the other clause are a simple subject, as also clauses composed of every mood of the verb save the Imperative.

This will be illustrated by the following examples.

	Subject.	*Predicate.*
Infin.	અજાણ્યાઓને શીખવવું	મને શારૂં લાગેછે

I like to teach the ignorant.

Indic.	હું ઈશ્વરનું ગનાન પામ્યો તે	મને શારૂં થયુ

It is a good thing for me that I have obtained the knowledge of God.

Contin. નીશાલ ચલાવે માટે કોઈ માંણુશ | મને જોઈયે

I want a man to conduct a school.

Involved subject. { પરમેસ્સરના પ્રેમથકી જે કામ કરીયે તે કાંમ એકલાં શારાં કેહેવાયે }

Actions can alone be called good, which we do from love tó God.

5. When of a sentence one clause contains the governing verb, and the other the object of the verb, the latter however complex in its nature precedes the former.

N. I. Hence, &c. see note 2. rule 1.

Note. As the correlate and definitive pronouns sustaining the burthen of sentences, are capable of becoming the objects as well as the subjects of the verb, the remark under rule 4 is applicable *mutatis mutandis* to this rule. One example will suffice.

Objective of the verb.

Ex. હમેશ શાચું બોલે એવા એક માંણુશને | મે હીંદુઓમાં જોયો નથી I have never seen among the Hindús, a man who would always speak the truth.

6. When of an interrogative sentence, one clause contains the subject matter of interrogation and the other the words which are the medium of interrogation, the former clause is placed first.

N. B. Hence, &c. see note 2. rule 1.

Ex. પોતાનો સભાવ બદલી શકે એવો કોણ છે? Who is there that can change his own nature?

7. When of a compound sentence, the one clause expresses action and the other clause the end to which the action is directed, the clause expressive of action is placed last.

N. B. Hence, &c. see note 2. under rule 1.

Ex. હું તમને ભણાવવા શારૂ આવ્યો છુઉં I have come to teach you.

Note. It is frequently requisite to express finality by the contingent mood, either in the former or latter clause. Neither can be placed in the latter clause, unless prefaced by the conjunction કે. If the ideas of finality are much involved and are contained in several sentences, then to avoid obscurity they are frequently placed in the latter clause. Speciality of design as regards the action, or the end of the action, can be expressed by the speaker by a stress of voice, but is not so easily expressed in composition. It may however be laid down as a general rule, that if the primary design be to express the end of action, the terms expressive of it are placed first either in the infinitive or in the contingent mood. If the primary design be to express action itself, the terms expressive of it are placed first, the end of action being expressed in a subsequent clause, headed by કે or એમાટે કે. If it be required to express very decidedly the end of action, some word denoting finality as એમાટે, precedes the verb expressing action, and કે connects the two clauses.

Ex. મે તેને એમાટે શીખામણ દીધી કે તે વળી એવું કાંમ ન કરે I have punished him to the intent that he might not do such a thing again.

8. When of a compound sentence, the one clause expresses the source or origin of action and the other the action, the clause expressive of the former is put first.

N. B. Hence, &c. note 2. rule 1.

Ex. હું ઘણું ચાલ્યો માટે થાકી ગયો I am tired because I have walked a great way.

Note 1. If the primary design be to express the action, and the subsidiary the source of the action, the sentence expressive of the former is placed first.

Ex. માહારો ભાઈ આવ્યો કેમકે તેને હીયાં કંઈ કામ છે My brother has come because he has some business here.

Note 2. If the primary design be to express the source of action, it is expressed in the former clause, a pronoun being placed before the word denoting origin.

Ex. લોકે તેને કાહાડી મુક્યો તે માટે હીયાં આવ્યો He came here because the people drove him away.

9. When of a compound sentence one clause expresses or involves any action relating to speech or thought, and the other

clause expresses the subject matter of such speech or thought, the former clause may be put first or last, as may be most suitable to circumstance and conducive to perspicuity.

N. B. Hence, &c. see note 2. rule 1.

NOTE. The subject matter of thought or of speech is expressed as nearly as possible according to the order of nature i. e. to what did actually transpire, whether in outward action or internal thought and feeling.

Hence the persons and tenses, &c. used, are frequently different from those used in English to represent the same fact, as will be seen at once by the following examples.

Ex. 1. તેણે મને કહ્યું કે હું માંદો છુઉં He told me he was sick.

2. મે જાણ્યું કે તે તરત શારો થશે I thought that he would soon recover.

3. તેણે મને કહ્યું કે માહારા ઘરમાંથી જાઓ He desired me to leave his house.

4. શાહેબ કેહેછે કે આજ માહારો જીવ શારો નથી Mr.—says that he is not well to day.

Excep. Where the use of the person corresponding to fact would necessarily lead to ambiguity, it is not employed.

Ex. શાહેબ કેહેછે કે હું શારો ચાકર છુઉં Mr.—says that I am a good servant.

Here the person originally employed was the second or third, but the use of either in this case would be ambiguous. The first is therefore employed.

IV. INTERLINEAR TRANSLATIONS.

*Extracts from Æsop's Fables.**

વાત. ૧. †

Word. 1.

કુતરો અને તેનું પ્રતીબીંબ.

Dog and him of Shadow.

એક કુતરો મોડા માં માંશ નો કડકો ઘાલીને નદી ઊતરીને પેલી તીરે
A dog mouth in flesh of piece having put in river crossing other side in
જતો હતો તેણે પોતાની છાયા પાણી માં દીઠી તારે તેના મન માં આવ્યું
going was him by own shadow water in saw then him of mind in came
કે આ કોઈ બીજો કુતરો માંશ નો કડકો લઈને જાએછે. તે હું એ ની
that this some other dog flesh of piece having taken is going that I him of
પાશે થી ખુંચી લઊં એવો વીચાર કરીને પોતાનું મોહોડું ઊઘાડીને
near from snatching will take such thought having made own mouth opening
લોભ થી તે લેવા ગયો તો મોહોડા માં નું માંશ પાણી માં પડ્યું તે
covetousness from it to take went then mouth in of flesh water in fell•it
તળે બેઠું તે ફરીને એને મળ્યું નહીં.
under sunk that again him to was found not.

---

* Although the original is in Bálbodh character, it is considered as assisting the early student unacquainted with that character to put it in the Gujaráti.

† For the sake of precision, words are disjoined, which in the original are connected.

શાર.

ESSENCE.

પરમેશ્વરે આપણુ ને જે આપ્યું તે માં શંતોશ ન માનીને જે પુરૂશ બીજા
God by us to what has given that in content not reposing what man other

નું લેવાને ઈછેછે તેને તે ન મલે અને પોતા ની પાશે જે હોય
of take to desires him to that not will be found and himself of near what may be

તે પણ જાય.
that also will go.

વાત. ૨.

Word. 2.

ખલદ અને દેડકું.

Bullock and Frog.

એક ખલદ ખીડ માં ચરતો હતો તાંહાં નાંનાં નાંનાં દેડકાં ફરતાં હતાં તેઓ
A bullock pasture in grazing was there small small frogs walking were them

માં નું એક દેડકું ખલદ ના પગ તલે ચંપાઈને મરીગયું તે વાત બીજે
in of one frog bullock of feet under being squeezed died that word other

દેડકે ઘેર જઈને પોતાની માને કેહી અને વલી બોલ્યું કે એવડો મોહોટો
frog by home going his mother to said and again said that so great

જીવ મે કોઈ દીવશે દીઠો નોહોતો તે શાંભલીને દેડકી પોતાનું પેટ
living thing me by any day on seen not was that having heard frog her belly

ઘણું ફુલાવીને બોલવા લાગી જે તે જીવ આવડો મોહોટો છે? દેડકો
much puffing out to say began that that living thing so big is? frog

બોલ્યો મા એ કરતાં ઘણો મોહોટો છે ફરીને તે થી વતું પેટ
said mother this than very big is again that from more belly

ફુલાવીને દેડકી બોલી આટલો છે? તે બોલ્યો મા તું પેટ ફુટે એટલી
puffing out frog said so great is? it said mother thou belly burst so much

ફુલે તોપણ તેના જેવડી થાયે નહીં તે શાંભલીને ગરવે કરીને ઘણુંજ
puff out yet it of so great will be not it hearing pride by from very much

ફુલવા લાગી એટલા માં પેટ ફાટીગયું અને તે મરીગઈ.
to puff out began so much in belly burst and she died.

શાર.
Essence.

ગરીબે પોતાની શક્તી પ્રમાણે ખરચ કરવું શ્રીમંત ની બરોબરી કરવા
Poor by own power according expense to make rich of imitation to make
જાયે તો દેડકી ની પઠે મારો જાયે.
he go then frog of way in he will be killed.

Extracts from the Panchopdkyan. Page 78.

વાત.
Word.

કોઈએક તલાવ માં કંબુગ્રીવ નામે કાચબો હતો તેના મીત્ર શંકટ ને
A pond in kămbŭgariv name by tortoise was him of friends Săngkat and
વીકટ નામે કરીને બે હંસ તે તલાવ ને કંઠે આવીને નીત્ય કાચબા શાથે
Vikat name by by two geese that pond to shore by coming daily tortoise with
સુખ દુખ ની વારતા કરે એક વરશ તે દેશ માં વરશાદ પડોનહી
pleasure pain of converse would make one year that country in rain fell not
એટલે વાવડી તલાવો બધાં સુકાઈગયાં તે શમે કાચબો હંસોને કેહેછે રે મીત્રો
so that well ponds all dried went that time tortoise geese to says oh! friends
પાણી વીના હું મરીજાઉં હવે કેમ કરીએ તે બોલ્યા રે ધીરજ નહીં
water without I shall die now how shall we do they said oh! patience not
મુક કહુંછે મોટા ઘાત ની વેલા એ પણ જે ધીરજ નથી મુકતો તે
do leave said is great destruction of time in even who patience not leaves him
ને ઊપાએ સુજેછે ને બીજું પોતાના મીત્ર ના કષ્ટ શમે જે કામે
to remedy appears and again own friends of calamity time in who use in

નહીં આવતો તે મીત્ર શા કામ નો? માટે તું કાંઈ ચીંતા નહીં કર હમે
not comes that friend what use of? wherefore thou any care not make we
કાંઈ ઊપાય શોધીકાહાડીયે પછી તે હંસો યે એક લાકડી લાવીને કાચબા ને
some remedy seek out after those geese by a stick bringing tortoise to
કેહું તું આ લાકડી ને મોડે થી વચમાં મજબુત પકડ ને બે છેડા હમે
said thou this stick to mouth by with middle in tight hold and two ends we
બે જણા પોતા ના વાંશા ઊપર મુકીને તમને લઈ—ઊડી—જાઈશે ને
two persons selves of shoulders on placing thee to taking arising will go and
જાહાં પાણી હશે તાંહાં મુકીયે પણ ખબરદાર જો મારગ વચે મોહું
where water may be there will place but take care if road middle in mouth
ઊઘાડશે તો તું જાણ્ કાચબે હા કહી ને હંસો તેને આકાશ
thou wilt open then thou know tortoise by yes said and geese him to sky
પંથે કરી લેઈ ચાલ્યા તે જોઈ એક શેહેર નાં માણસો એકઠાં થયાં ને
road in by taking went that seeing a city of men together were and
આંગલી કરીને એક બીજા ને દેખાડેછે રે જુયો જુયો શું અચરત છે જે એક
finger making one other to shows oh! see see what wonderful is that a
લાકડી ને બે પંખી વલગ્યા છે ને વચમાં કંઈ ચકર સરખું દીશેછે તે
stick to two birds stuck are and middle in something ring like seems that
લોક ની મંડલી જોઈ કાચબા ને ધીરજ નહીં રહી તે વારે પેલા
people of assembly seeing tortoise to patience not remained that time in those
લોકો શા કાજે મલા છે એમ હંસો ને પુછવા લાગ્યો એટલા માં લાકડી
people what for met are so geese to to ask proceeded so much in wood
થી મોહું છુટી-ગયું ને હેટલ પડ્યો તેને લોકે તરત મારી-નાંખ્યો.
from mouth got loose and below fell it to people by soon killed.

Extracts from the Bál Mitra.

લક્ષમણ્.

Lákshman.

એક ઘણો ગરીબ સંતાજી એવે નામે મજુર હતો તેને નાંનાં નાંનાં છ
A very poor Săntaji such name by labourer was him to little little six

છોકરાં હતાં તેઓનું પેટ કેમ ભરાશે માટે એક દાહાડો તેને ઘણી
children were them of belly how shall be filled therefore one day him to much

ચીંતા થઈ તે માં બીજું એવું થયું જે તે વરશ માં અંન શારૂં પાક્યું નહીં
anxiety was it in other such was that that year in grain well ripened not

માટે આગલા વરશ કરતાં દાંણો બમણો મોંઘો થયો. સંતાજી રાત દાહાડો મેહનત
therefore preceding year than grain twice dear was. Săntají night day trouble

કરે તોપણ છોકરાં ને જાડા પાતલા રોટલા પેટ ભરીને ખવાડવાને પુરા પૈશા
would make yet children to coarse thin bread belly filling give to eat to full pice

તેને મલે નહીં એવો તે ઘણો દુખ માં પડ્યો. એક દીવશ તેણે
him to would be found not so he much suffering in fell. one day him by

પોતાનાં શઘલાં છોકરાં ને પાશે બોલાવ્યાં અને આંખો માં આંસુ આંણીને કેહેછે અરે
own all children to near called and eyes in tears bringing says oh

માહારાં વાહાલાં છોકરાં હોણ દાંણો મોંઘો ઘણો છે હું આટલી મેહેનત કરૂંછું
my dear children this year grain dear very is I so much labour make

તોપણ તમારૂં પેટ. ભરાય એટલો દાંણો મને મલતો નથી એવી માહારી
yet your belly be filled so much grain me to is found not such my

અવસ્થા છે તમે જુયો જે શઘલા દાહડા ની માહારી મજુરી આટલા એક રોટલા
condition is you see that all days of my hire so much one bread

માં ખરચ થાયછે માટે મને જેટલું મલેછે તેટલા માં નીરવાહ
in expended is therefore me to as much as is findable so much in management

તમારે કરવો જોઈશે બીજો કશો ઊપાય નથી અને એટલે તમારાં પેટ
you by make must other any remedy not and so much by your bellies

ભરતાં નથી તે ખરાં પણ વારૂં જીવતા બચશો એટલું બોલીને
are filled not that true but well alive you will be saved so much having spoken

તે છાંનો રેહ્યો. તે બચારા થી આગલ બોલાયું નહીં અને તે આંખો ઊંચી
he silent remained that poor by onward was speakable not and he eyes high

દેવ ના શામીયો કરીને રોવા લાગ્યો તે જોઈને છોકરાં પણ રોવા લાગ્યાં
God of opposite making to weep began that seeing children also to weep began

અને પોત પોતાના મન માં કેહેવા લાગ્યાં હમે ગરીબ હમે નાંહાંનાં હમે

and each self of mind in to say began we poor we little we

અભાગીયાં હમારા ઊપર દયા કર હમારા બાપને શાહે થા હમને ભુખે

unfortunate us on pity make our father to help be oh! us to hunger from

મરવા દેઈશ નહીં.

to die do let not.

Extracts from the Gospels.

ઈહોનનો શુભ વરતમાન.

John of Glad Tidings.

પેહેલો અધ્યો.

First Chapter.

૧. આરંભે શબ્દ હુતો ને તે શબ્દ ઈશ્વર ની પાશે હુતો ને તે શબ્દ

1. beginning in word was and the word God of near was and the word

ઈશ્વર હુતો. ૨. તે આરંભે ઈશ્વર ની પાશે હુતો. ૩. તે થી શઘલું પેદા

God was. 2. it beginning in God of near was. 3. him by every made

થયું ને જેકાંઈ પેદા થયું તે તે ના વીના પેદા થયું—નોહોતું. ૪. તે

was and whatever made was that him of without made been not was. 4. him

માં જીવન હુતું ને તે જીવન માણશ નું અજવાળું હતું. ૫. ને તે અજવાળું

in life was and the life man of light was. 5. and that light

અંધારા માં થયું પણ અંધારાએ તે ને માન્યું નહીં. ૬. ઈહોન નામે ઈશ્વર

darkness in was but darkness by it to received not. 6. John name by God

થી મોકલાએલો એક માણશ હુતો. ૭. તે શાહેદી લીધે આવ્યો કે

from sent a man was. 7. he testimony to on account came that

અજવાલા શબંધી તે શાહેદી આપે એ શારૂ કે તેંથી શંધાં વીશ્વાશ

light concerning he testimony might give this for that him by all belief

કરે. ૮. તે અજવાલું તે પોતે નોહોતો પણ તે અજવાલા શબંધી ની

might make. 8. that light he self not was but he light concerning of

શાહેદી આપવા આવ્યો. ૯. જગત માં જે કોઈ આવે તેહેને પ્રકાશ
testimony to give came. 9. world in who any may come him to light
કરનાર તેજ ખરૂં અજવાલું હુતો. ૧૦. તે જગતમાં હુતો ને જગત તેથી પેદા
maker that true light was. 10. he world in was and world him by made
થઈ-હુતી પણ જગતે તેહેને ઓલખ્યો નહીં. ૧૧. તે પોતાનામાં આવ્યો પણ
been had but world by him to knew not. 11. he own in came but
પોતાનાયે તેહેને માન્યો નહીં. ૧૨. પણ જેટલાઓયે તેહેને માન્યો
own by him to received not. 12. but as many by him to received
તેટલાઓનેં એટલે તેહેના નામપર વીશ્વાશ કરનારાઓને તેણે ઈશ્વરના દીકરાઓ
so many to that is him of name on belief makers to by him God of sons
થવાનો અધીકાર આપ્યો ૧૩. જેઓ લોહીથી નહીં તથા દેહે કરીને નહીં
becoming of authority gave. 13. who blood from not and body by by not
તથા માણુશની ઈછાથી નહીં પણ ઈશ્વરથી જનમ પામ્યા. ૧૪. શબ્દ દેહ-
and man of desire from not but God from birth received. 14. word body-
ધારી થયો ને આપણામાં રેહ્યો ને હમે તેનો મહીમા જોયો ક્રીપા તથા શાચ્યપણુ
taker was and us in lived and we him of glory saw grace and truth
શંપુરણ બાપના એકના-એક દીકરા ના જેહેવો મહીમા હુતો. ૧૫. તે શબંધી
perfect father of only one son of as glory was. 15. him respecting
ઈહોને શાહેદી આપી ને શાદ પાડીનેં કેહ્યું કે જે શબંધી મે કેહ્યું
John by testimony gave and voice raising said that whom concerning me by said
હુતું કે માહારી પાછલ જે આવનારો છે તે માહારી અગાઊ હુતો તે એજ છે
had that me of behind who comer is he me of before was he this is
કેમકે તે માહારા પેંહેલાંજ હુતો. ૧૬. ને તેહેની શંપુરણતાથી આપણે શંધા
because he me of before was. 16. and him of fullness from we all
ક્રીપા પર ક્રીપા પાયેમા છઈયે. ૧૭. કેમકે મુશાની હસ્તક શાસ્ત્ર અપાયું
grace on grace received have. 17. because Moses of through law was given
પણ ઈસુખ્રીસ્ત થી ક્રીપા તથા શાચ્યપણુ આવ્યાં. ૧૮. ઈશ્વર ને કોઈયે કદી જોયો
but Jesus Christ by grace and truth came. 18. God to any by ever seen

નથી એકનોએક દીકરો જે બાપ ની છાતી આગલ છે તેણે તેહેને ઓલખાવ્યો.
not only one son who father of breast before is him by him to made known.

૧૯. જેવારે યહુદીઓઓ એ યરૂશાલેમ માંથી યાજકો ને તથા લેવીઓ ને યોહાન
19. what time at Jews by Jerusalem in from priests to and Levites to John

પાશે પુછવા મોકલ્યા કે તમે કોણ છો તેવારે જે શાહેદી તેણે પુરી
near to ask sent that you who are that time in what testimony him by fulfilled

તે એ છે કે. ૨૦. તેણે કબુલ કીધું ને ઇંકાર કીધો નહીં પણ કબુલ
that this is that. 20. him by confess made and denial made not but confess

કીધું કે હું ખ્રીસ્ત નથી.
made that I Christ not.

*The above expressed by Roman Characters.**

1. árămbhé ṣăbda hato né té ṣăbda íṣvar ní pásé hato né té ṣăbda íṣvar hato. 2. té arămbhé íṣvar ní pásé hato. 3. té thí săghalúng pédá tháyúng né jé kángí péda tháyúng té téna víná péda tháyúng, nohotúng. 4. té máng jívăn hatúng né té jívăn màṇaṣnúng ajválúng hatúng. 5. né té ajválúng ăndhárámáng tháyúng paṇ ăndhárâé té né mányo nahí. 6. íhon nàmé íṣvar thí mokláélo ék màṇaṣ hato. 7. té sáhédí né lídhé ávyo ké ajválá samăndí ní sáhédí púré é sárú ké té thí săndháng vísvás karé. 8. té ajválúng té poté nohoto paṇ té ajválá samăndi sáhédí ápavá ávyo. 9. jăgăt máng jé koé ávé té né prakás karnár té kharúng

1. The unaccented a is sounded as a in *A*merica. When accented thus ă, it is sounded short as u in cup. When accented thus á, it is sounded as á in the French *la*. When accented thus à it is somewhat broader.

2. ú is never sounded short but as oo more or less lengthened.

3. í is not sounded short as the English, but as long e or ee. When accented shus ĭ, it is sounded as i in fin.

4. é is the English a in *name*, more or less lengthened when not accented it is short as e in jem.

5. ng final is merely a soft nasal.

6. o is always long as in bone.

* Let the student carefully observe, that in conformity with the Alphabet :—

ajválúng hato. 10. té jägät máng hato né jägät té thí pédá tháé hatí
paṇ jägäté té né olkhyo nahí. 11. té potáná máng ávyo paṇ potánáé
té né mànyo nahí. 12. paṇ jétláoé té né mànyo étlé té ná nàm par
vísvás karnáráo né téo né ísvar ná díkráo thaváno adhíkár ápyo.
13. jéo lohí thí nahí tathá déhé kariné nahí tathá màṇaṣ ní íchá thí nahí
paṇ ísvar thí jänäm pámyo. 14. né ṣäbda dédhárí tháyo né ápṇáng
máng réhyo né hamé téno mahíma joyo kripá tathá sáchpaṇ sämpúrna
bápná eknáék díkrá ná jévo mahíma hato. 15. íhoṇé té samändí ṣáhédí
ápí ké jé samändí mé kahyúng hatúng ké máhárí páchal jé ávnáro ché
té máhárí agàú hato té éj ché kemké té máhárá péhéláng hato. 16. né
té ní ṣämpúrṇta thí ápṇé sändhá kripá par kripá pàmya chaíyé.
17. kemké músa ní hästäk ṣástra apáyúng paṇ. ísú khríst thí kripá
tathá sáchpaṇ ávyáng. 18. íṣvar né koíé kädí joyo nathí éknoék
díkaro jé báp ní chátí ágal ché té né té né olkhávyo. 19. jé váré
íhudíoé írúsalém máng thí yájako né tathá lévío né íhon pásé púchavá
moklyá ké tamé koṇa cho té váré jé ṣáhédí té né púri té é ché ké.
20. té né kabúl kidhúng né ínkár na kídho paṇ kabúl kídúng ké húng
khríst nathí.

માથીઉ નો શુભ વરતમાન.

Matthew of Glad Tidings.

પાંચમો અધ્યો.

Fifth Chapter.

૧. ને તે લોકો ને જોઇને પાહાડ પર ગયો ને તે બેઠો ' એટલે
1. and he people to seeing mountain on went and he was seated at that time
તે ના શીશ્યો તે ની પાશે આવ્યા. ૨. ને તેણે તેઓ ને પોતા ના મોહો
him of disciples him of near came. 2. and him by them to self of mouth
થી ઉપદેશ કીધો કે. ૩. દીન આતમા વાલાઓ ને ધન છે
with instruction made that. 3. humble spirit them that have to blessing is
કેમકે સ્વરગ નું રાજ તેઓ નું છે. ૪. શોક કરનારાઓ ને ધન
because heaven of kingdom them of is. 4 mourning makers to blessing

છે કેમકે તેઓ દીલાશો પામશે. ૫. જે રાંકડા છે તેઓ ને ધન છે
is because they consolation shall find. 5. who meek are them to blessing is

કેમકે તેઓ દેશ નો વારશો પામશે. ૬. જે નીતી ના ભુખ્યા
because they country of inheritance shall find. 6. who righteousness of hungry

તથા તરશા છે તેઓ ને ધન છે કેમકે તેઓ ત્રપત થશે. ૭. જે
and thirsty are them to blessing is because they satisfied shall be. 7. who

દયાલુ છે તેઓ ને ધન છે કેમકે તેઓ દયા પામશે. ૮. શુધ મન
merciful are them to blessing is because they mercy shall find. 8. pure mind

વાલાઓ ને ધન છે કેમકે તેઓ દેવ ને જોશે. ૯. શલાહ કરાવનાર ને
that have to blessing is because they God to shall see. 9. peace makers to

ધન છે કેમકે તેઓ દેવ ના દીકરાઓ કેહેવાશે. ૧૦. નીતી ને
blessing is because they God of sons shall be called. 10. righteousness to

લીધે જેઓ ને લોક શતાવેછે તેઓ ને ધન છે કેમકે સ્વરગ નું
on account who to people persecute they to blessing is because heaven of

રાજ તેઓ નું છે. ૧૧. જાહારે લોક માહારે લીધે તમને મેહેણું
kingdom them of is. 11. when people me to on account you to insult

મારશે ને તમારી પુઠે લાગશે ને તમારા ઊપર હરેક તરેહ ની ભુંડી વાત
shall strike and you behind shall stick and you on every kind of evil word

જુઠી કેહેશે તારે તમને ધન છે. ૧૨. તમે ખુશ થાઓ, ને ઘણા હરખાઓ
false shall say then you to blessing is. 12. you glad be and very be glad

કાંજે તમારે સ્વરગ-માં ફલ ઘણું છે, કેમકે તમારા-થી-અગાઊ-ના-ભવીશ-
because to you heaven in reward much is because you from before of future

કેહેનારાઓ-ને એમજ શતાએવ્યા. ૧૩. તમે પ્રથવી-નું મીઠું છો; હવે, જો મીઠું
sayers to thus persecuted. 13. you earth of salt are now if salt

નીસ્વાદ હોએ, તો તે થી કેમ મીઠું થાએ; તે બાહાર ફેંકી—દેવા, ને લોક-ના પગ
tasteless be then it by how salt can be it out throw away and people of feet

તલે ચંપાઈ—જવા=વીના, બીજા કાંઈ કામનું નથી. ૧૪. તમે પ્રથવી નું અજવાલું
under to be trodden except other any use of not. 14. you earth of light

છો પાહાડ પર નું શેહેર છાનું રેહી શકતું નથી. ૧૫. ને દીવો કરીને વાશણ
are hill on of city secret remain can not. 15. and light having made vessel
તલે કોઈ મુકતું નથી પણ દીવી પર મુકેછે તે થી તે નું અજવાલું શંધાં
under any places not but candle-stick on places it from it of light all
ઘરનાં ને પડેછે. ૧૬. તેમ તમે તમારૂં અજવાલું લોક ની આગલ એવું
house of (them) to falls. 16. so you your light people of before so
પ્રકાશ કરો કે તેઓ તમારી રૂડી કરણીયો જોએ ને સ્વરગ માંના તમારા બાપ
light make that they your good works may see and heaven in of your father
ની સ્તુતી કરે. ૧૭. તમે એમ ન શમજો કે હું શાસ્ત્ર ને તથા ભવીશ
of praise may make. 17. you thus not understand that I law to and future
કેહેનારાઓ ની વાતો ને ખંડન કરવા આવ્યો છઉં ખંડન કરીનાખવા આયેવો
sayers of words to frustrate to make come have frustrate to make come
નથી પણ હું થાપન કરવા આયેવો છું. ૧૮. કેમકે હું તમને નીએ કહુંછઉં કે
not but I stable to make come have. 18. because I you to certainly say that
આકાશ ને પ્રથવી ગુજરી-જાએ તાહાં-શુધી શાસ્ત્ર માંનો એક કાહાનો કે માત્ર પણ શધું
sky and earth pass away there up to law on of one jot or tittle even all
શીધ થયા વીના જનાર નથી. ૧૯. માટે એ શેહેજ આજ્ઞાઓ
accomplished been without goer not. 19. wherefore these light commands
માંની એક પણ જો કોઈ તોડશે ને માણસો ને તેમ શીખવશે તો સ્વરગ ના
in of one even if any shall break and men to so shall teach then heaven of
રાજ માં તે કનીષ્ટ કેહેવાશે પણ જો કોઈ તેઓ ને પાલશે ને તેમ
kingdom in he lowest shall be called but if any them to shall keep and so
શીખવશે તો તે સ્વરગ ના રાજ માં શ્રેષ્ટ કેહેવાશે. ૨૦. કેમકે
shall teach then he heaven of kingdom in best shall be called. 20. because
હું તમને કહુંછું કે શાસ્ત્રીયો ની તથા ફારીશીઓ ની નીતી કરતાં જો તમારી
I you to say that scribes of and pharisees of righteousness than if your
નીતી શારી ન હોએ તો સ્વરગ ના રાજ માં તમે જશો નહીં.
righteousness good not be then heaven of kingdom in you shall go not.

*The above expressed by Roman Characters.**

1. né té lokoné joíné páhád par gayo né té béṭho èṭlé téná síso té ní pásé ávyá 2. né té né téo né potáná moho thí úpdés kídho ké. 3. dín atmá váláo né dhăn ché kemké svrăg núng ráj téo núng ché. 4. şok karanárao né dhăn ché kemké téo díláso pàmaşé. 5. jé rángkadá ché téo né dhăn ché kemké téo dés no váraso pàmaşé. 6. jé níthí ná bhúkhá tathá tarsá ché téo né dhăn ché kemké téo trăpta thaşé. 7. jé dayálú ché téo né dhăn ché kemké téo dayá pàmaşé. 8. şúdh măn váláo né dhăn ché kemké téo íşvar ní drasṭí pàmşé. 9 salá karnáráo né dhăn ché kemké téo íşvar na díkaráo kéhévaşé. 10. nítí né lídhé jéoné lok satávé ché téo né dhăn ché kemké svărag núng ráj téo núng ché. 11. jáháré lok máháré lídhé tămané ménáng máraşé né tămárí púṭhé lágaşé né tămárá úpar harék taré ní júṭhí vát kéhéşé táháré tămané dhăn ché. 12. tamé khúş tháo né ghaná harkháo kémké tamáré svărag máng phăl ghanúng ché kemké tamárá thí agàú ná bhavís kéhénáráo né téoé emaj satávyá hatá. 13. tamé prathaví núng míthúng chó havé jomíthúng nisvád tháyung to té thí kém míthúng tháé té báhár phengkí dévá né lok ná păg talé chămpáí javá víná bíjá kángí kám núng nathí. 14. tamé prathaví núng ajválúng cho páhád par núng şéhér chánúng réhí săkatúng nathí. 15 né divo karíné vásan talé koí múkatúng nathí pan díví par mukéché té thí ajválúng săndháng ghar náng né padéché. 16. tem tamé tamárúng ajválúng évúng prakáş karo ké téo tamarí rúdi karnío joé né svărag máng ná tamárá báp ní stútí karé. 17. tamé om na sămjo ké húng sástrá né tathá bhavís kéhénáráo ní váto né khăndăn karavá ávyo chúng khăndăn karavá ávyo nathí pan húng thápan karavá ávyo chúng. 18. kémké húng tamané nísché kahúng chúng ké ákás né prathaví gujarí jáé táháng súdhí şastra máng no ék káháno ké mátra pan săndhúng sídh tháyá víná jánár nathí. 19. máṭé é séhéj ágnáo máng ní ék pan jo koí todasé né mànaso né tem şíkhavasé to svărag ná ráj máng té kănísht kéhévâşé pan jo koí téo né pálé né tém şíkhavaşé to té svărag ná ráj máng saréshṭ kéhéváşé. 20. kemké húng tamané kahúng chúng ké şástrío ní tathá phárísio ní nítí karatáng jo tamárí nítí şárí na hoé to svărag ná ráj máng tamé jaşo nahí.

---

* See power of vowels.

V. FAMILIAR PHRASES

Rendered into Gujaráti, in Native and Roman Characters.

Where are you going?	તમે કાંહાં જાઓછો ?	tamé káháng jáocho ?
Whence have you come?	તમે કાંહાંથી આવ્યા ?	tamé káhángthí ávya ?
Call the servant	ચાકરને બોલાવો	chákarné bolávo.
This sugar is not clean	આ ખાણુ સાફ નથી	á khán̤ s̤áph nathí.
Bring more from the bazar	બજાર માંથી બીજું લેઈ આવો	bajár mánthí bijúng léi ávo.
Who told you so?	તમને કોણે કહ્યું ?	tamané kon̤é kahyúng ?
Do you know where he lives?	તમે જાણોછો કે તે કાંહાં રેહે છે ?	tamé jàn̤ocho ké té káháng réhéché ?
	તેનું રેહેવાનું ઠેકાંણું તમે જાણો છો ?	ténúng réhévánúng ṭhékánúng tamé jàn̤ocho ?
I do not know	હું જાણતો નથી	húng jàn̤ato nathí.
	મને માલુમ નથી	mané màlum nathí.
Bring a towel	રૂમાલ લાવો	rumál lávo.
Call a washerman	કોઈ ધોબીને બોલાવી લાવો	koí dhobíné bolávi lávo.
Take me into the Fort	મને કીલામાં લેઈ જાઓ	mané kilámáng léi jáo.
Call a palkee and four hammals	એક પાલખી ને ચાર ભોઈઓને બોલાવો	ék pálkhí né chár bhoío-né bolávo.
How many bearers do I require?	કેટલા ભોઈઓ જોઈયે ?	kéṭlá bhoío joíyé?
Four are enough	ચાર ઘણા છે	chár ghan̤á ché.
I don't know the road to	નો રસ્તો મને માલુમ નથી	no răsto mané màlum nathí.

Direct me	મને રસ્તો બતાવો.	mané răsto batávo.
This rice is not clean	આ ભાત ચોખો નથી	á bhát chokho nathí.
Wash your hands	તમારા હાથ ધુઓ	tamárá háth dhụo.
I want a servant	માહારે એક ચાકર જોઈયે	máháré ék cháker joíyé.
Do not let any body come	કોઈને આવવા ન દો	koíné ávavá na do.
Whom have you served?	તમે કોણની ચાકરી કીધી?	tamé konní chákari kídhí?
What is your name?	તમારૂં નામ સું છે?	tamárúng nàm súng ché?
Can you cook?	તમને રાંધતાં આવડે છે?	tamané rándatáng avadé ché?
Bring a chair	ખુરચી લાવો	khúrchí lávo.
I will give you ten rupees a month	હું તમને દશ રૂપીઆ મહીનો આપીશ	húng tamané dăṣ rúpia mahíno ápiṣ.
That is quite enough	તે ઘણું છે	té ghaṇúng ché.
He is ill	તે માંદો છે	té mándo ché.
Do as you please	તમારી ખુશી પ્રમાંણે કરો	tamári khúṣi pramàṇé karo.
Say, I am not well	કોહો કે માહારો જીવ શારો નથી	koho ké máháro jív ṣáro nathí.
I have fever	મને તાવ આવેછે	mané táv avéché.
You must take some medicine	તમારે ઓશડ કરવું જોઈયે	tamáré osaḍ karavúng joíyé.
Shall I read to you?	હું તમને વાંચી શંભળાવું?	húng tamané vànchí ṣămbhalávúng?
We shall have rain	વરશાદ આવશે	varṣád ávaṣé.
There is no air in the room	આ ઓરડીમાં કંઈ વા આવતો નથી	á ordímáng kangí vá ávato nathí.
What can we get here to eat?	હીયાં સું સું ખાવાને મળે	hiáng ṣúng ṣúng khávàné mălé.
Send for some plantains	કેળાં મંગાવો	kéláng măngávo.

Go and see	જાઈને જોજો	jainé jojo.
Listen to what I say	હું કહું છું તે શાંભળો	húng kahúngchúng té sàmbhalo.
Be quiet	છાના રોહો	chháná roho.
Clean my shoes	માહારા જોડા શાફ કરો	máhárá jodá ṣáph karo.
Make the coffee and bring it	કાફી બનાવી લાવો	káphí bănávi lávo.
Come quickly	વેહેલા આવો	véhélá ávo.
See who is there	જુઓ કે કોણ છે	júo ké koṇa ché.
Is this water good to drink?	આ પાણી પીવાને શારૂં છે ?	á paṇi pivàné ṣarúng ché?
Bring me some soap	કંઈ શાબુ લાવો	kangi ṣábú lávo.
Bring water for a bath	નાહાવાને પાણી લાવો	náhávàné paṇi lavo.
Ask him his name	તેનું નામ પુછો	ṭénúng nàm púcho.
Where do you live ?	તમે કાંહાં રોહોછો ?	tamé káháng rohocho ?
Bring more rice	બીજો ભાત લાવો	bíjo bhát lávo.
Loose the dog	કુતરાને છોડીદો	kútaráné choḍí do.
What shall we do now?	હવે આપણે શું કરીયે ?	havé ápṇé súng karíé ?
There are no more cups	બીજાં પેયાલાં નથી	bíjáng péyáláng nathí,
You have not brought enough	જેટલું જોઈયે તેટલું લાવ્યા નથી	jéṭlúng joiyé teṭláng lávyá nathí.
That is right	તે ઠીક છે	té ṭhík ché.
Do not trouble me	મને તસદી ન દો	mané tăsdí na do.
I am very busy	માહારે ઘણું કામ છે	máháré ghaṇúng kám ché.
Can you read ?	તમને વાંચતાં આવડે છે ?	tămané vànchatáng ávadé ché ?
Do you speak English?	તમને અંગરેજી બોલતાં આવડેછે ?	tămané ănggréjí bolatáng ávadé ché ?

Where is his house ?	તેનું ઘર કાંહાં છે ?	ténúng ghar káháng ché?
What kind of man is he ?	તે કેહેવો માણસ છે ?	té kéhévo màṇaṣ ché ?
Put this book in its place	આ ચોપડી ઠેકાણે મુકો	á chopaḍí ṭhékàṇé múko.
Sit on the floor	ભાંગે પર બેશો	bhángé par béṣo.
Move this table	આ મેજ બીજે ઠેકાણે મેલો	á méj bíjé ṭhékáṇé mélo.
Bring this couch this side	આ કૌચ યેણીગમ લાવો	á cauch yéṇí găm lávo.
Why have you been so long ?	તમને એટલી વાર કેમ લાગી ?	támané eṭlí vár kém lágí?
I want to go out	માહારે બાહાર જવું છે	máháré báhár javúngché.
I have not time now	હમણાં મને ફુરશદ નથી	hamaṇáng mané phúrṣăd nathí.
Is Mr.— at home ?	શાહેબ ઘેર છે ?	ṣáhéb ghér ché ?
I shall not keep this servant	આ ચાકરને હું નહી રાખીશ	á chákarné húng nahi rákhíṣ.
What is this called in Gujaráti ?	ગુજરાતીમાં આને શું કેહેછે?	gujarátí máng áné súng kéhéché ?
Put out the lamp	દીવો હોલવો	dívo holavo.
Light the lamp	દીવો શલગાવો	dívo salgávo.
Pay the bearers	ભોઈઓને પઈશા આપો	bhoíoné paisá ápo.
Get the carriage ready	ગાડી તઈઆર કરો	gáḍí taiár karo.
Is it time to go ?	જવાને વખત છે કે નહી ?	javáné văkhăt ché ké nahí ?
Saddle your master's horse	શાહેબના ઘોડાપર જીન બાંધો	ṣáhébná ghoḍá par jín bándho.
Come back quickly	પાછા જલદી આવો	páchá jaldí ávo.
Bring a light	દીવો લાવો	dívo lávo.
What o'clock is it ?	કેટલા વાગા ?	kéṭlá vágyá ?
You do not do this right	આ કામ તમે ઠીક કરતા નથી	á kám tamé ṭhík karatá nathí.

Lay down the carpet	શેતરંજી પાથરો	ṣétrănjí pátharo.
Bring some bread	રોટલી લાવો	roṭalí lávo.
Shew the book to me	મને ચોપડી દેખાડો	mané chopaḍí dékháḍoi
Bring your account book	તમારા હીશાબની ચોપડી લાવો	tamárá hisábní chopaḍ. lávo.
Give me your account	તમારો હીશાબ મને આપો	tamáro hisáb mané ápo.
Have you spent all the money?	તમે બધા પઈશા ખરચી ચુકા?	tamé bădhá paisá kharachí chúká?
Mr.—is gone for a walk	શાહેબ ફરવા ગયો	ṣáhéb pharavá gayo.
Mr.—is gone in the carriage	શાહેબ ગાડીમાં બેશીને ગાયો	ṣáhéb gáḍimáng béṣíné gayo.
Give my compliments to Mr.—and say	શાહેબને માહારી શલામ કોહો ને બોલો કે	ṣáhébné máhári ṣalám koho né bolo ké.
Mr.—is gone out on horse-back	શાહેબ ઘોડાપર બેશીને ગયા	ṣáhéb ghoḍá par béṣíné gayo.
Have you any money?	તમારી પાશે પઈશા છે?	tamári páṣé paiṣá ché?
Give this man four rupees	તે માણસને ચાર રૂપીઆ આપો	té màṇasné chár rúpíá ápo.
What has happened to you?	તમને શું થયું છે?	tămané súng thayúng ché?
Clean the furniture	શામાન શાફ કરો	ṣámán ṣaph karo.
I do not understand	હું શમજતો નથી	húng ṣămăjato nathí.
My pronunciation is not good	માહારો ઊચાર શારો નથી	maháro uchár ṣáro nathí.
The table is broken	મેજ ભાગીગઈ	méj bhágí gai.
I am in a hurry	મને ઊતાવલ છે	mané utával ché.
Never mind	કંઈ ચીંતા નહીં	kăngi chintá nahí.
Is any body there?	તાંહાં કોઈ છે?	táháng koi ché?

This cup is cracked	આ પેયાલું તડકી ગયું	á péyálúng taḍkí gayúng.
I have no money	માહારી પાશે પઈશા નથી	máhárí pásé paisá nathí.
I will give it you to morrow	હું કાલે તમને આપીશ	húng kálé tămané ápis.
Come the day after to morrow	પરમ દાહાડે આવજો	param dáhádé ávjo.
Call the carpenter	સુથારને બોલાવી લાવો	sútbárné bolávi lávo.
How broad is this cloth?	આ લુગડાનો પનો કેટલો છે?	á lúgadá no păno kéṭlo ché?
Enquire what is the price of grain	દાણાની કીમત પુછો	dáṇání kímăt púcho.
My servant is gone out	માહારો ચાકર બાહાર ગયો	máháro chákar báhár gayo.
Pull the punká	પંખો ખેંચો	păngkho khéncho.
Explain to me	મને શમજાવો	mané sămjávo.
Teach me Gujaráti	મને ગુજરાતી ભણાવો	mané gujaráti bhaṇávo.
Do you know the English language?	તમને અંગરેજી ભાશા આ-વડેછે?	tămané ănggréjí bhása ávadéché?
If I make a mistake, tell me.	જો હું ચુક કરૂં તો મને કોહો	jo húng chúk karúng to mané koho.
I saw him yesterday	મે કાલે તેને જોયો હતો	mé kálé téné joyo hato.
Bring two seers of milk	બશેર દુધ લાવો	basér dúdh lávo.
Do this every day	રોજ રોજ કરો	roj roj karo.
Pay the postage	ટપાલના પઈશા આપો	ṭapálná paisá ápo.
Take this letter to the Post Office	ટપાલમાં આ કાગલ લેઈ-જાઓ	ṭapálmáng á kágal léí jáo.
Have the horse shod	ઘોડાને નાલ બંધાવો	ghoḍáné nál băndhávo.
Go on with your work	તમારૂં કામ કર્યા જાઓ	tamárúng kám karyá jáo.
You have made a mistake	તમે ચુક કીધી	tamé chúk kídhí.

Come back quickly	જલદી પાછા આવો	jáldí páchá ávo.
Go early in the morning	શવારે વેહલા જજો	ṣaváré véhélá jajo.
Procure it as it is wanted	જોઈતું જોઈતું મંગાવો	joítúng joítúng măngávo.
Do not get it all at once	શામટું લેવું નહીં	sámṭhúng lévúng nahí.
This tea is not good	આ ચાહ શારી નથી	á cháh ṣárí nathí.
What is the price of this box?	આ પેટીની કીમત શી છે ?	á péṭíní kímăt sí ché?
Where is the padlock of this box?	આ પેટીનું તાળું કાંહાં છે?	á péṭínúng tálúng ḳáháng ché?
Get dinner ready	ખાણું તૈઆર કરો	kháṇúng taiár karo.
Seven persons are to dine	શાત માણશો જમનારાં છે	ṣát màṇaso jămnáráng ché.
Remain in waiting	હાજર રોહો	hájar roho.
Tell him to stop a little	તેને કોહો કે શબુર રાખો	téné koho ké ṣăbur rákho.
Who wrote this letter?	આ કાગલ કોણે લખ્યો ?	á kágal koṇé lăkhyo?
What is the cost of this?	આની શી કીમત છે ?	ání sí kímat ché?
What is the day of the week?	આજ કહો વાર છે ?	áj kahyo vár ché?
What is the day of the month?	આજની શી તારીખ છે?	ájní sí táríkh ché?
This is the sixth day of the month	છઠી તારીખ છે	chaṭhí tárikh ché.
Let him go	તેને જવા દો	téné javá do.
Whose servant are you?	તમે કોણનો ચાકર છો ?	tamé koṇno chákar cho?
Speak the truth	શાચું બોલો	ṣáchúng bolo.
Come next week	આવતે અઠવાડીએ આવજો	ávaté aṭvádié ávjo.
Wake me in the morning	શવારે મને જગાડજો	ṣaváré mané jagáḍjo.
You have come very late	તમે મોહોડા આવ્યા	tamé mohoḍá ávyá.

I do not like this	આ મને શારૂં લાગતું નથી	á mané sárúng lágatúng nathí.
Come at the right time	વખત પર આવજો	văkhăt par ávjo.
Do this carefully	આ કામ ખબરદારીથી કરો	á kám khăbardárithí karo.
Take care of the child	છોકરાને શંભાલો	chokaráné sămbhálo.
Stop the gádi	ગાડી રાખો	gádi rákho.
Bring fish for breakfast	નાશતા શારૂ માછલાં લાવો	nástá sárú máchaláng lávo.
Tell him to sit down	તેને બેશાડો	téné bésádo.
I am coming directly	હું હમણાં આવું છું	húng hamanáng ávúng chúng.
I will come after dinner	હું જમીને આવીશ	húng jămíné ávis.
Bring some hot water	હુનું પાણી લાવો	húnúng pàni lávo.
This water is not hot	આ પાણી હુનું નથી	á pàni húnúng nathí.
Bring cotton for bedding	ગોદડીને શારૂ રૂઊ લાવો	godadíné sárú rúú lávo
Bring a maund of cotton	એક મણ રૂઊ લાવો	ék man rúú lávo.
Come and visit me	તમે મને મલવા આવજો	tamé mané mălavá ávjo.
I shall be glad if you visit me	તમે મને મળો તો ઘણું શારૂં	tamé mané mălo to ghanúng sárung.
He was to come but he has not come	તે આવવાનો હતો પણ તે આવ્યો નથી	té ávaváno hato pan té ávyo nathí.
This man cheats very much	આ માણસ ઘણો દગો કરેછે	á mànas ghano dago karéché.
He is not to be trusted	એનો કાંઈ ભરોશો નથી	éno kángi bharoso nathí.
Do you understand what I say ?	હું કહુંછું તે તમે શમજો છો?	húng kahúng chúng té tamé sămjocho ?
Open all the windows	શઘલી બારીયોને ઊઘાડો	săghali báríoné úghádo.

This bungalow is very good	આ બંગલો ઘણો શારો છે	á bănggalo ghaṇo sáro ché.
What is its rent?	તેનું ભાડું કેટલું છે?	ténúng bháḍúng kéṭlúng che?
Five majúrs are wanted	પાંચ મંજુરો જોઈયે	pánch majúro joíyé.
Four carts are required	ચાર ગાડાં જોઈયે	chár gáḍáng joíyé.
Hired bullocks are wanted	ભાડેના બલદ જોઈયે	bhádéná băläd joíyé.
I write him a letter	હું તેના ઊપર કાગલ લખી મોકલીશ	húng téná úpar kágal lăkhí moklíṣ.
I want a boat to go to Surat	સુરત જવા શારૂ એક બતેલો જોઈયે	Súrat javá sárú ék batélo joíyé.
I wish to go to morrow	કાલે માહારે જવું છે	kálé mahárè javúng ché.
What you will take for this?	એનું શું લેશો	énúng súng léṣo.
That is very cheap	તે ઘણું શસતું છે	té ghaṇúng ṣastúng ché.
Your goods are very dear	તમારૂં શામાન ઘણું મોંઘું છે	tamárúng ṣámàn ghaṇúng mongghúng ché.
We are going to take a walk	હમે ફરવા જઈયે છઈયે	hamé pharavá jaiéchaíyé.
Dismiss him	એને રજા આપો	éné razá ápo.
Dinner is on the table	ખાણું મેજ પર છે	kháṇúng méj par ché.
Have you dined?	તમે જમી રહ્યા?	tamé jămí rahya?
I want a pen and ink	સાઈ કલમ જોઈયે	sái kălăm lávo.
He is come back	તે પાછો આવ્યો છે	té pácho ávyo ché.
I dine out to-day	આજ હું બાહાર જમવા જાઉં છઉં	áj húng báhár jamava jáúng chúng.
Do that work well	તે કામ શારી પઠે કરો	té kám ṣárí pathé karo.
Speak softly	ધીમે ધીમે બોલો	dhímé dhímé bolo.
Shut that door	તે બારણું બંધ કરો	té bárṇúng bandh karo.
Open this door	આ બારનું ઊઘાડો	á bărnúng úghádo.
Keep it always open	હમેશ ઊઘાડું રાખો	hamés úghádúng rákho.